THE
AGILE
MIND

THE
AGILE
MIND

HOW YOUR BRAIN
MAKES CREATIVITY
HAPPEN

ESTANISLAO
BACHRACH

1 3 5 7 9 10 8 6 4 2

Virgin Books, an imprint of Ebury Publishing,
20 Vauxhall Bridge Road,
London SW1V 2SA

Virgin Books is part of the Penguin Random House group of companies whose
addresses can be found at global.penguinrandomhouse.com

Penguin
Random House
UK

First published in the United Kingdom by Virgin Books in 2016
First published in Argentina by Random House Mondadori S.A. in 2012

www.eburypublishing.co.uk

A CIP catalogue record for this book is available from the British Library

ISBN 9780753556863

Printed and bound in Great Britain by Clays Ltd, St Ives PLC

Penguin Random House is committed to a sustainable future for
our business, our readers and our planet. This book is made from
Forest Stewardship Council® certified paper.

Inspired by Goyo
To Victoria, Uma and Valentin

TABLE OF CONTENTS

PROLOGUE

The last ten years have seen some fascinating technological advances in the field of neuroscience. In particular those aimed at achieving a greater understanding of the brain and its intimate relationship with the mind. For the very first time, we are able to see the electrical impulses inside our head that allow us to create new connections using pathways established by our experience. Using neuroimaging techniques we can photograph thoughts and measure neuron activity as the brain works to solve a problem.

We have reached a key moment in our understanding of everything we know about how we function, who we are, and the nature of our human brain. As I hope to show in this book, such an understanding will help us to improve the quality of our lives in a variety of ways; I am convinced that we can only change our brain by knowing how it works. The Agile Mind aims at debunking some of the myths surrounding the brain, the often mistaken ideas we have about it, and cultivating the things we know in ways that will help us to become more creative. Creativity can appear to spring from nowhere, as if by magic. We are now starting to understand how that creative magic works, and the deeper our understanding of it, the better we will be able to make it work for us.

You may not know it, but neuroscience already plays an important role in our lives – although scientific jargon can sometimes be an obstacle to accessing the exciting insights that field provides into the world and us. My desire as a scientist is to take the reader on a guided tour of some of the most inspired research carried out by experts in the field of creativity and neuroscience, both past and present. It is easy to show through today's advanced technology how we are able to continue to learn and be more creative right up until the day we die. My aim is for the reader to experience this for themselves, and at the same time to realise that aside from the ability to solve problems, resolve conflicts, and do well at work, being more creative means having a more fulfilling, enjoyable life.

We live in a globalised society where products and services increasingly resemble one another, to the extent that it is often hard to tell them apart. Technology and technical expertise are ever more easily and cheaply available, whether in Singapore, China, Cyprus, the United Kingdom or the United States. Much of the knowledge that was so prized and sought after in the twentieth century no longer represents a challenge. In order to excel in today's world, businesses, governments and organisations require people to be creative. And it is the most empathic and creative among us who make the most difference in society, economics, education and industry. Logical thinking, as we understand it, is necessary but insufficient. Organisations are keen to employ people who can empathise with others (clients, fellow employees, colleagues, partners or students), who have a greater understanding of others' needs, concerns, tastes, expectations, what satisfies them; who are able to think creatively and innovatively and can offer different services or products, a better experience. However, people like this are in short supply in our society.

From the earliest beginnings of our educational system up to the present day, the emphasis has always been on the importance of logical analysis and deductive reasoning (which prevailed during the twentieth century) as opposed to our capacity for creativity and empathy. However, these latter qualities are essential if we are to triumph in the twenty-first century, and it is up to us to nurture them in ourselves, regardless of who we are or what we do for a living. People who are curious and courageous are promoted and rewarded and become indispensable in any organisation. It is those able to come up with alternative solutions to societies' problems, both big and small, who truly make their mark.

In this book I will draw on current scientific advances and research into our brain/mind, so that the reader can get to know it as never before. I will also suggest alternative ways, in the form of exercises based on that research, to increase creative capacity in everyday life.

Moving on a bit. If we observe any child under the age of six, it becomes obvious that human beings are creative from the moment they are born. But then school and society gradually demand we stop using those neural pathways and focus primarily on others: logic and analysis, which become our dominant thought patterns. Up until a few years ago, scientists believed that creativity in young people and adults was a lost cause, that neurons and synapses which aren't used are lost for ever. The good news is that today's scientists have shown very specifically that this is untrue. As I said before, *the brain has the power to regenerate and to carry on learning until the day we die*. We can all be more creative if we employ the right techniques and methods to stimulate those neurons and their connections, which most of us have scarcely used. Think of the brain as a muscle, and our lives as training for a race; if we spend most of our time exercising only one part of that muscle, the rest will atrophy. But now we know that with discipline, determination and exercise, the atrophied muscle can be made to work again. If we choose to make this journey, we will end up discovering that we are more creative, and that we can use this ability to improve our quality of life.

The Agile Mind is about our most precious mental resource: our capacity to imagine things that are entirely new, and to be creative. We often think of creativity as something in-built that only happens to others, and which doesn't involve us much. And yet our lives are defined by human creativity: your mobile phone, your favourite poem, the comfortable chair you are sitting in as you read, the central heating that protects you from the cold, that song which reminds you of a loved one, the pill you take when you have a headache.

The Agile Mind is an invitation to a brain spa, where you can learn to nurture, cosset and coax your mind and your creativity back into shape.

INTRODUCTION

One sunny Sunday in Buenos Aires, my daughter and I were playing her favourite game on the swings. She was two at the time, and would happily spend the best part of an hour sailing backwards and forwards through the air, occasionally tilting her head to look up at the sky. I liked to push the swing from the front so I could watch the permanent smile on her face as she fully enjoyed the moment. Every few minutes, in my naive, adult way, I would suggest she have a go on the slide or the seesaw, assuming she must be getting bored. I couldn't understand how she could spend so much time on it. Obviously, I was using my timescale, not hers. Every now and then, I would stop pushing the swing to check my smartphone for emails, browse the newspaper online, or send a message. I did this strategically so that before the swing lost momentum and she had to ask me, I would resume pushing, and her curly locks would once more flutter against the back of the seat. Then, all of a sudden, it happened: 'Papa, no phone,' she said, still beaming. I walked behind her and carried on pushing the swing from there, doing my best to dissimulate while continuing to use the touchscreen on my mobile. Three minutes later, this time without the smile or the 'Papa', she shouted: 'No phone!' I slipped the mobile back in my pocket, reluctantly yet guiltily. Uma had sensed that I wasn't a hundred percent there with her, and she was right. She taught me an important lesson, and from then on I chose not to take my mobile phone to the park any more. Each time we set off, I would show Uma that I was leaving it on the living room table, and she was much more contented as we walked the seven blocks to the local park.

I think it happened to me on our third trip to the park without my mobile phone. Uma now preferred me to push her on the swing from behind. My arms moving rhythmically back and forth lulled me into a sort of trance. Suddenly, ideas started tumbling into my head; I could see them, feel them, appearing randomly one after the other, too fast for me to respond. What to do that weekend, how to present a project to a client, how to prepare a new class, even how to invent a new shower feature or make the playground equipment in the park safer for kids. And so on ad infinitum. When Uma commented about a pigeon or another toddler in the park, or asked me for a sweet, it took me several seconds to reply, to emerge from that cloister of ideas. However, she seemed to enjoy my momentary confusion. She laughed and exclaimed: 'Papa! Papa! Are you crazy?'

As we walked home that afternoon, I realised I had forgotten most of the ideas that had come to me while I was pushing my daughter on the swing. Some had vanished without trace, others I knew were related to a client, although I couldn't remember exactly how.

As I lay in bed that night, I knew I'd had a lot of thoughts in that park, including some that were commonplace and unexceptional, but also others that were more unusual: 'creative' or new to me. And yet I couldn't remember any of them. I soon forgot the incident, until the next time I pushed Uma on the swing and the same thing happened. Twice in a row couldn't be coincidence. With my scientific background, I resolved to find out what was going on, and from then on, each time I pushed Uma on the swing and the rhythmical movement began, with her smiling face and her golden curls, I waited attentively to be enveloped by my private flow of ideas. Needless to say, any conscious attempt to make it happen ended in failure.

I have frequently heard speakers at international business conferences affirm that ninety percent of all new innovative products and services we enjoy come from ideas thought up by 'ordinary' employees outside working hours. Like me at the swings with Uma.

I have spent many years studying innovative businesses, and after speaking to a lot of interesting employees on every level of the job hierarchy and from different cultures, companies, industries and countries, I have reached the same conclusion: *new ideas can arise at any time, but they tend to occur more frequently the more relaxed we are.* According to the law of probabilities, the more ideas we have, the more likelihood one of them will be good, better, fresh, creative and different. Some people call this *reverse brainstorming*: instead of asking our brain to generate ideas for two hours on a Tuesday afternoon because our boss says so, we make the most of the fact that our mind works twenty-four hours a day, three hundred and sixty-five days a year. And we already do: we all have at least one or two places, times or situations during the day (in the car, in the shower, in bed, in the bathtub, cooking, doing sport, playing, meditating, sleeping) when our consciousness is bombarded with ideas. On the advice of employees in highly innovative organisations, of artists, including engineers at Toyota, I started to carry a small notebook with me to the park so that I could write down my ideas immediately.

We now know that we forget the majority of our thoughts, including any new ideas we might have. Amazingly, Uma doesn't mind her papa 'drawing' in his little notebook, as she refers to it, while pushing her on the swing; on the contrary, she also brings her pad along so that she can draw and share an authentic father–daughter moment. That notebook has become part of my body, and I put any projects I want to remember under a heading, as opposed to jotting down ideas as they occur to me, making it much easier to find something I want to reread.

It is 5 September 2011. I am sitting in El Dorado airport in Bogotá waiting to board a flight back to Buenos Aires. I leaf through my notebook, and every ten or twenty pages I come to a fresh heading printed in capital letters, followed by an almost-illegible scrawl: my ideas. Among my current projects are: **classes in Mendoza, conference in Cartagena, talk at Coca-Cola, neuromarketing, Costa Rica 2011, Sarmiento the innovator, miscellaneous projects, executive education.** During this downtime at the airport, I rethink some of my ideas. Projects have a limited lifespan in my notebook and, pen in hand, I browse through some of those that have already happened and are now cluttering up my field of vision, and I draw a line through them. While doing this, I come to the heading: 'miscellaneous projects', and a sentence catches my eye; at some point, I don't remember when, I increased it to the power of ten, which in my private language means I have revisited an idea many times, and given it a great deal of thought.

For example: 'Write a book[10]', it says in bold letters, almost scoring the paper.

The time has come. So here I go.

> *The act of writing down our creative challenge can spark creative ideas. We have to put it down on paper.*

BREAKING OLD PATTERNS

Genes and memes

No matter who you are, you can change your mind. It all depends on you. No matter how creative you or others think you are, you can improve on that. Creativity gurus have long been telling us how to enhance our creativity, based on their own experience or intuition and with more or less good results. Today, drawing on the most advanced technology, neuroscience has shown clearly and concisely that our brains are capable of learning and changing until the day we die – a capacity known as neuroplasticity. Regardless of past experiences or genetic make-up, our minds, i.e. the way we use our thoughts, can change the structure and anatomy of our brain. When you start reading this book, your brain will be one way, with a particular set of neural connections. By the time you finish reading, your brain will have changed, made fresh connections or pathways, and it will doubtless be a better brain, because you will have learned to recognise its potential, as well as some of its limitations. And if, in addition, you methodically apply the techniques I will be proposing throughout the book, your creative potential will increase in ways that are noticeable not just to you but also to your colleagues or fellow students, to your family members and friends. I observe and experience these incredible changes not only in myself (I am and have always been my own guinea pig), but also in the hundreds of people whom I have the privilege and pleasure to work with in a number of different organisations. I wish to share this knowledge with you, dear reader, to help you to become more creative and to enjoy a more fulfilled and therefore a happier life.

How did we humans get to where we are? We could say that we are still on earth thanks to two continuous movements: biological evolution and culture. We evolve biologically according to random mutations in our genes, and those mutations that favour survival in the environment are then selected by nature in a process called natural selection, which occurs beyond our consciousness or control. Where culture is concerned, our creativity plays the biggest role, generating enormous changes in our cultural paradigms in a process that occurs on an entirely conscious level.

Consequently, creativity could be considered the cultural equivalent of the genetic changes that lead to our evolution.

We now know that due to certain mutations, some of us evolve a nervous system in which the discovery of new things, essential to the development of creativity, stimulates the brain's pleasure centres. That's to say, just as some people might be passionate about sex or food, others have evolved to become passionate about, and to derive pleasure from, learning new things. However, it appears this propensity towards newness, discovery and exploration doesn't only depend on a genetic component, but is also influenced by childhood experience. If that is true, then our ancestors, who recognised the importance of innovation, would doubtless have protected and learned from these creative individuals, whose inventiveness enabled them to be better prepared to face unforeseeable circumstances and threats to their survival.

And yet, a far more primitive and powerful force than creativity also played an important role in human survival: entropy – or conserving our energy. Basically we conserve energy when there are no external demands on us, and this is when entropy plays an important part in the control of our mind and body. Our need to conserve energy is so great that we instantly associate leisure time with relaxation. Going for a walk in the park, watching a movie, reading a book or simply contemplating the ceiling. Switching to automatic pilot. Not using up our energy. It is as if we humans were being tugged at by two opposing instructions from our brain: on the one hand to use the minimum effort necessary (entropy) and on the other to explore and search for the new (creativity).

Entropy seems to exert a stronger pull on most of us than the pleasure of discovering fresh challenges or new ideas. However, fortunately, some people respond much more strongly to the rewards of discovery. Nevertheless, regardless of which of these two instructions you identify with more, or in what area or moment of your life it occurs, creativity is always extremely pleasurable and makes us feel good.

To sum up: we are born with two somewhat contradictory sets of instructions. On the one hand we are programmed to conserve our energy – the basic instinct of self-preservation. And on the other, we are oriented towards being more expansive, exploring and enjoying novelty and taking certain risks – the curiosity all children possess. It is the second that leads to creativity. Despite the need for both 'programmes', we can achieve the first without much effort, assistance or motivation. The latter, being creative, is difficult to cultivate alone. As adults, we have few opportunities to be curious in our work or in our everyday lives. There are too many things preventing us from taking risks or exploring, and the motivation needed to behave in more creative ways quickly fades. This is due, in large part, to the fact that most of us don't feel or think of ourselves as creative.

Genes are automatically passed on from generation to generation, but the same isn't true of inventions or ideas. Every child has to learn from the beginning how to use fire, the wheel or nuclear energy. These units of information, which we are required to learn so that our culture survives, are known as 'memes' – a term coined by Richard Dawkins in his book *The Selfish Gene*. The values of all our memes, from language and numbers through to theories and laws, have to be passed on to our children in order not to be forgotten. In cultural terms, then, memes could be considered as equivalent to genes.

It is possible for an extremely creative individual to change a meme. And if a sufficient number of people think that this change constitutes an improvement for society, it becomes a new part of the culture. New songs, new ideas, new machines; this is what creativity is about. But memes don't arise automatically, as occurs in biological evolution when genes mutate. That's to say, a price has to be paid so that creativity can occur. It takes effort and energy to change traditions, and involves learning. Learning requires us to pay attention – a limited resource – to the information we are given. We are incapable of processing large amounts of new information simultaneously, and as we are constantly busy and rushing about, we have few opportunities to think up new ideas. Most of our time is taken up with the task of survival, the everyday activities of work and home life.

In other words, we need to free up a lot of attention in order to be highly creative, or just more creative, in any given discipline or environment. If we are constantly busy, we are unlikely to come up with fresh ideas that might change or improve a product, a song, or a way of life. We need to devote our attention to our creative challenge.

A definition: creativity is the mental activity whereby at any given moment a revelation or insight occurs in the brain resulting in a new idea or action that has value. It means breaking with habitual thought patterns, which we all do more or less frequently. If we look at ideas that are going to change paradigms or memes within a tradition, culture or discipline, we will see that the decision about whether or not they were new and valuable comes from people who are knowledgeable about the medium or discipline in which the idea or action is attempting to gain ground. Consequently, once they approve and accept the idea, it will have undergone a kind of social evaluation that says: 'This is truly creative'. And so, creativity doesn't only exist in someone's head, but also in the interaction of thoughts within a sociocultural context. It is a systemic rather than an individual phenomenon.

Other definitions of creativity: someone who expresses thoughts that are unusual, and who is passionate and inspired; people who experience the world in a fresh or original way; people who have a different view of the world and who are less judgemental, who are open to having particular insights that allow them to generate ideas, or products or actions which lead to important discoveries.

Lighting up new pathways

Imagine for a moment that we are on the top floor of a tall building from which we are able to contemplate a sprawling city at night. If we look more closely, we might notice that some areas are lit up. If we are able to glimpse any cars, we might also see that only a few streets are illuminated by streetlights or car headlamps. Our brain is a bit like a city that is mostly in darkness, but where a few avenues, roads and streetlights are always illuminated.

Extending the analogy, our brain possesses a huge potential to be illuminated. We could switch on numerous streetlamps (neural connections) and yet few streets (neural pathways) are lit up, connected and in constant use. This underlines the fact that we have a tendency to use the same information when trying to solve any problem. That's to say we look in those few illuminated streets for what we already know, have seen and experienced, even though other, more poorly lit streets or avenues containing fresh material, ideas or creative solutions are always open to us.

It is as if we are living on semi-automatic-pilot, and the majority of our responses to dilemmas and challenges come from our experiences, certainties and culture. Indeed, we could say that these are the names of the three main streets that are permanently illuminated.

Let's remember that our brain, by means of entropy, is a great conserver of energy. It has always been and it is still helpful to our survival to keep some in reserve in case of unexpected events where we might find ourselves in a fight or flight situation. That is why, when faced with an intellectual challenge, we initially look for solutions in what we already know.

We live from experience, which is a constant source of information. But if we want to find new forms and ideas, if we want to be inspired, to have insights in order to build something creative, we need to make an effort to illuminate and connect other neurons. Effort implies using energy. If we succeed, we will be able to discover several possibilities and responses to the same question, dilemma, goal or challenge. We will refer to these from now on as *creative challenges*.

> The more clearly you see the nature of your creative challenge and what it is, the easier it will be for you to find a solution. Imagine your creative challenge as the completed jigsaw on the cover of the box; without it you would be hard pressed to assemble the puzzle.

When we get up to go to work, school, university, or wherever we go in the morning, how do we get there? We always or almost always take the same route. The same roads or side streets, the same underground or bus. We could take two, three, possibly four, different routes to get where we are going each morning. But why use different roads or buses if we know (*certainty*) that we can get there by taking the same route (*culture and experience*)? The brain doesn't like to use energy on things it already knows. It contains thought patterns and structures that become established in our neural pathways as time passes and we accumulate more experiences – like the illuminated streets of our city. As we shall see, the creative process *liberates* those patterns and structures making way for the *possibility* of different thoughts.

I don't think, therefore I am

> The brain is a wonderful organ; it starts working the
> moment you get up in the morning and does not
> stop until you get to the office.
>
> Robert Frost

At primary school, children start spending less time playing. Our education is based on processing information about things that have already happened, about the opinions of a lot of people who are no longer alive, and about what exists today. That's to say, most of our responses are based on learned information. 'Reply' and 'response' share the same etymological root; responses are the prayers given for the dead, and there is something lifeless about the replies we give. The problem with it is that we are no longer thinking. We are being taught how not to think. In other words, the moment we believe we know the answer to something based on our education is the moment when our own thoughts die. And that is why so many of us have difficulty using our imagination and creativity to develop new ideas. Our ideas are structured in powerful and predictable ways into very specific categories and concepts. To think creatively we need to generate associations and connections between two or more different ideas. By doing so we can create new categories and concepts, only we aren't taught to process information in this way.

Brain warm-up techniques designed by Edward de Bono to generate associations between two or more completely unrelated subjects:

▲ Choose four random words.
Invent a reason to discard one.
Example: Dog, cloud, water, door.
Reason 1: Dog, water and door fit into a house, but a cloud doesn't.
Reason 2: Dog, cloud and door contain the letter 'o' but water doesn't.

More techniques:

▲ Choose six random words and divide them into two groups of three. Each group must have its own selection criterion.

▲ Make two random lists (A and B) containing four words each. Find a reason for associating a word from list A with a word from list B.

Continued

- Make a list of five random words.
  Select one of those words and find a reason for associating it with each of the other four words.
- Choose two random words.
  Combine them in such a way that you can create a business out of them.
  Add a third random word. Think about how that third word could be used to obtain more profits from your business.
  Add a fourth random word.
  Now think about how this fourth word might help to make your business environmentally friendly.
- Choose five random words.
  Find a reason to decide which is the most expensive, useful, dangerous, attractive, long lasting, cheap etc.
- Choose five random words.
  Select two that will be the ends of a bridge.
  Begin to relate the words in such a way that each has a reason to be associated with the word on the right.
- Choose two random words.
  Use those words to depict a murder scene.
  Add three random words. Each of them should be a clue to the murder.
  Out of those clues construct a theory as to how the murder took place and, if possible, who is the culprit.
- Choose four random words.
  Find a reason to select two out of the four that are somehow contradictory.
- Choose four random words.
  Using those exact four words (not derivative or associated words) invent a newspaper headline.
  Write a summary of the headline.

In other words, chemically speaking, we think reproductively; we confront new problems based on past events or solutions. Unconsciously we ask ourselves: what do I know about this problem based on my experience, my education or my work? The brain then analyses and selects the most promising approach, thereby excluding other possibilities. It moves clearly and persistently towards a solution based on past perspectives. This is what we refer to as 'dominant thought patterns'. It is important to acknowledge that these patterns also simplify life's complexities: our ability to do our job, to drive a car or get on a bicycle without falling off are all achievable thanks to these unconscious thought patterns which allow us to process complex data.

Two groups of a hundred university students are given the following task:

Group 1: You are seven years old and today your school is closed. You have the whole day to yourself. What would you do? Where would you go? What would you look at?

Group 2: You have the whole day to yourself. What would you do? Where would you go? What would you look at?

The two groups have ten minutes in which to write their answers, and afterwards they are given a series of brainteasers and creativity tests; for example, finding an alternative use for an old car tyre. Group 1, who for a moment imagined they were seven again, performed much better in the brainteasers, and generated twice as many ideas in the creativity test than those in group 2.

We can recover our lost creativity by pretending we are children again.

To think creatively is to think productively. When we are confronted with a dilemma, we should ask ourselves how many different ways there are of looking at the problem, rethinking it to solve it, rather than how to tackle it based on what we already know. The idea is to try to find different answers, many of which might be very unconventional, and a few of which might even be exceptional. Habitual reproductive thinking leads to very rigid thought patterns, which often prevents us from solving a problem. Generally speaking, when we think reproductively, the responses we come up with are almost identical or at least superficially similar to past experiences. Reproductive thinking produces dull, not very original ideas. If you think the way you have always thought, you will come up with the same old ideas.

Six word technique

What is the essence of your creative challenge? Can you write it in a sentence containing only six words?

'Customers want to consume my product.' 'Complete all my projects before March.' 'How lucky I never got married.' Etc.

Reducing a complex problem to a simple six-word sentence stimulates the imagination.

A form of creative thinking known as conceptual blending allows us to generate associations and connections between different ideas. As we will see later, in order to achieve this, we must liberate our thoughts to allow the space for new possibilities.

Children are experts at conceptual blending. When we are young, our thoughts are like a glass of water: inclusive, fluid and clear. Everything is mixed up together and can combine in ways that generate multiple connections and associations. That's why kids are spontaneously creative. And yet at school we are taught to define, divide, segregate and label things into different categories. For the rest of our lives these categories remain separate, they never combine. It's as if the fluid thinking of children becomes frozen, like ice cubes in a tray, each cube representing a category; our thoughts become frozen.

> 'Every child is an artist. The problem is how to remain
> an artist once we grow up.'
>
> Pablo Picasso

Conceptual blending, a history

When examining great inventions, both past and present, we might ask ourselves: are we more creative today than we were a hundred thousand years ago? But what about fire, the spear, the wheel, the canoe, agriculture…?

Mankind's first great creative idea was perhaps rubbing two stones together to produce fire. I can imagine those early humans seeing lightning strike a tree during a storm, setting it on fire, and the wind helping spread the flames across the African plain. I can also imagine them banging stones together to scare predators away. As they did so, they would occasionally notice sparks fly. Those humans (who, unlike most of us, hadn't received a formal education) were practising conceptual blending. The stones producing sparks, the lightning setting fire to the trees, the wind making the flames spread. They blended these concepts and produced fire with their own hands, by rubbing sticks and stones together. There were no schools to teach them how to make fire; there were no scientists, artists or philosophers, nothing to structure their imagination, which remained absolutely pure. They thought the way they had been born to think, i.e. naturally and spontaneously. They were able to combine conceptually the different essences, functions, characteristics and patterns they perceived in the environment in which they lived. Some anthropologists, for example, think that early humans were inspired by observing spiders' webs to create nets to snare animals and for fishing. The same process of conceptual blending led them to integrate bones, flint and wood to make tools, or weapons for hunting and killing their prey. During that era, they did paintings and drawings that narrated their experiences. And that is how art was born.

One plus one equals one

Let's return to the present and observe logical thought patterns in action. Imagine I am confronted with a creative challenge: 'Ideas for improving swimming pools, or how swimmers experience swimming pools'. Because I already know (from learned experience) precisely what a swimming pool is, my dominant thought patterns will unfreeze the ice cube labelled 'swimming pools' in order to try to find a solution to my challenge. No matter how many times I unfreeze that ice cube, the most I will achieve, or create, is a slight improvement. My resources are limited specifically to what I have learned about swimming pools and swimmers. Now, imagine if I were to unfreeze a different ice cube, one labelled 'cranes', for example, and place it in the same glass with the ice cube labelled 'swimming pools'. If they melt at the same time, and combine, they will become fluid. One plus one equals one, not two. By mixing that water I am beginning to associate and connect many more possibilities which are much more creative. I might think up a swimming pool that can lift into the air, a steel pool, or one with pulleys which is moveable. Conceptual blending can have an extraordinary effect, and in many cases will generate entirely novel, creative ideas. We could even go as far as to say that creativity arises in any discipline – whether in art, science or technology, or in everyday life – when the mind can blend totally different concepts and ideas. What's more, if we look back at the most creative ideas in human history, we will see that they always come from a combination of old ideas; in other words, novel ways of combining what we already know.

We are educated to think logically and analytically, and consequently we find it extremely difficult to associate things that are seemingly unrelated – like swimming pools and cranes. This lack of ability to associate disparate concepts is a huge obstacle to being creative. We build mental walls separating different concepts, ice cubes in their individual little trays.

Conceptual blending

Write down the names of five people you love most in the world, then look at the first letter of each name. For example, the 'M' from Mary, the 'A' from Alex and so on.

Quickly write down any object that comes to mind beginning with each of those letters: for example, monkey, airplane, etc.

Pair the objects to create something new. For example, monkey plus airplane equals a banana-shaped plane.

Besides conceptual blending, another way of liberating thought patterns in order to achieve creative ideas is to think in terms of essences and origins. To get rid of the words, categories and labels for the objects and things around us, just as our distant African cousins lived.

For instance, the essence of a car is to transport people, and that of a toothbrush to clean teeth. The origin of a disposable razor is a sharp blade. Let's say my challenge is to find ways of 'improving savings accounts'. The technique would be to think about the essence of a savings account: 'to keep people's money safe for the future', for example. Let's think what other things people and animals keep safe: squirrels keep food for winter, warehouses keep goods safe, hangars keep planes safe, and so on. Now we can start to associate and combine all those things to see whether we can't come up with new ideas to improve savings accounts. For example, in winter (associating with the squirrel), the bank could offer a higher interest rate to encourage people to save more money when it's cold.

Another similar technique is to become part of the problem. Using the same example of the savings account, let's imagine we are a savings account. You are the place where people keep their money. What would you say to the banker? What would you say to the customer? How or where would you like to be? Inside or outside? Big or small? Or multi-coloured? As you start to answer, imagining in this case that you are the savings account, new ideas will arise.

All three techniques – conceptual blending, the essence or origin of a challenge and becoming part of the problem – are ways of introducing randomness in order to break the patterns of logical thinking.

I am the problem

Imagine that you are the problem in your creative challenge, or part of it.

Look at the situation from that perspective: how would I feel if I were the challenge? What would it mean to me? How would I feel if I were this idea I am developing? What advice would I give myself?

The essence of the challenge

If your creative challenge is to lead a more peaceful, relaxed life, ask yourself: What things are peaceful? What things are relaxed? What moves slowly? Tortoises? All right, what is the origin or essence of a tortoise? And from there, start to make associations and come up with ideas for your challenge.

Continued

Thinking in terms of origins and essences frees the imagination from the obstacles or traps that words, categories and labels can sometimes create.

The origin of the challenge

If my creative challenge is to improve car washes, I might make a list of all the other things we wash (hair, clothes, streets, nails, dogs, etc.). The source of the problem is 'washing', 'to wash', 'cleaning'.

Generate connections, links, associations, which you can adapt to your car wash.

Leonardo da Vinci was the first to write about the importance of introducing randomness in order to be able to create different thought patterns from those established by education and experience. Da Vinci came up with wonderful ideas inspired by unrelated or random objects. His challenge was to combine them conceptually with his dilemmas. He might have looked at the stains on a wall or the ashes left in a grate, the shapes of clouds or the patterns in mud. One of the most interesting things about these techniques is that when we concentrate on two objects, concepts or ideas, no matter how different or apparently unrelated they are, the brain will find a connection. The explanation for this phenomenon is metaphors. If we say: 'what the eye doesn't see the heart doesn't grieve over', everyone immediately knows what it means. And yet, the eye and the heart aren't directly related.

There is no logical connection in this sentence, and yet we understand it. What our mind is doing is taking two distinct, unrelated concepts and blending them: *If we can't see something we can't feel sad about it.*

Leonardo da Vinci technique

Leonardo maintained that until we see something from three or four different perspectives, we cannot truly understand it. A complete, true understanding only comes from merging all those perspectives into one.

For example, when he designed the first-ever bicycle, he thought about the challenge from the point of view of transport (what would be best technically speaking), of the backers (who might finance the prototype and production of these bicycles), of the consumer (who would use them) and of the cities (where the bicycles would be ridden). Then he synthesised all of these perspectives to create his final design.

Studies in educational psychology show how, as well as an awareness of the essence/origin of things and becoming the problem, multiple perspectives generate increased creativity.

So, based on the idea of conceptual blending, we can begin to use the technique of combining problems; superimposing one challenge on which we are working onto another. Sometimes one problem will 'contaminate' or 'infect' another, allowing us to associate and relate the ideas contained in both. Generally speaking, we are used to resolving one problem and then going on to the next. A useful tip is to see what happens if we try to tackle two problems at once.

Let's imagine we are building a house of cards, as we often did when we were younger. The house starts to grow in a completely predictable way until suddenly, without warning, it reaches a critical balance point and collapses. The same thing happens when we introduce a random object, concept or idea into our imagination and combine it with our creative challenge; it's quite possible that, at some point, completely randomly and without warning, it will stimulate a thought that causes some neurons to light up and connect, creating a chain reaction as other, neighbouring, neurons do the same. Just as the cards collapse onto one another when the house topples, this avalanche of mental activity will spread to other, smaller neural networks. Just as the house of cards has one structure before it collapses and another one afterwards, our thoughts start to construct themselves until they reach a critical point where they regroup to form new ideas.

Nature is, without doubt, the most significant creative force of all. We have always been taught that nature is astonishingly productive, that it creates vast numbers of species through trial and error and then, through a process of natural selection, decides which ones will survive. It is thought that ninety-five percent of species disappear. In time, the genetic storehouse that survive the environmental conditions begin to stabilise. These genes undergo mutations, which slowly generate variations in species. Species whose genetic storehouse contains no variations will be unable to adapt to changes in the environment and, as a result, those creatures will tend to disappear. Variety is essential in nature. A similar process occurs in our brain. We have the capacity to create ideas, and we do this largely based on our pre-existing thought patterns (genetic storehouse). These patterns were formed according to our experience. However, if we fail to vary those patterns (mutations) all our ideas will end up being similar or identical and will lose the adaptive advantage (disappearance of the species).

Yesterday I was giving Uma, who is three years old, a bath, and at one point she said to me: 'Papa, pass me those two spoons.' And I replied: 'There aren't any spoons, we're in the bathroom.' And in my head I thought: 'spoons are in the kitchen'. She insisted: 'Papa, Papa, pass me the spoons, please, I'm playing, I want the spoons.' She gestured with her hand towards what were actually a couple of toothbrushes. In her imagination anything is possible; because it is still unstructured, it hasn't yet incorporated the concepts and categories that start to be constructed in childhood and, in particular, at school. When we are children we have a tendency to extend rather than eliminate possibilities. At that age, besides being extremely creative, we take great joy in exploring, which is essential in the encouragement of creativity. What alternative name might you give the first chapter of this book? Why?

BRAIN/MIND

I thought I saw a lovely leopard

When our brains became fully formed a few hundred thousand years ago, the world was an extremely hostile place. We went out hunting in order to survive. Due to environmental conditions and the predators that wandered the earth, we were more or less on permanent alert: looking out for food, but also taking great care not to be eaten ourselves. At that time our most feared predator was the leopard.

As we have seen, the brain evolved efficiently to conserve plenty of energy in case of an unexpected threat to our existence. In general, the women cared for the children, gathered fruit and seeds, and the odd rodent, and they too were on the alert. Those men or women who didn't have that reserve of energy in their brain, and were unable to escape or defend themselves against unexpected attacks, probably ended up being eaten. That's to say, they were less likely to have any descendants.

Try the following exercise: close your eyes and think about a sunset for thirty seconds, then open your eyes and describe how and where it was. It's possible (dare I say, certain) that you thought about a sunset you have already seen, at the beach, in the mountains, in the countryside – a further example of how the brain doesn't like to waste energy on something it already knows. If you give the brain's hard drive a command, it will search, among those illuminated streets, for the known, which requires very little or no effort. Most people's brains, when they command it to show them a sunset, will dredge up one from their store of familiar sunsets, rather than waste fresh neurons imagining a new one. Being creative isn't easy, then: it takes effort to connect the seemingly unconnected, to travel down dark or poorly lit streets. This is the journey we are making in this book.

As we start getting to know our brain, how it has evolved, its limitations and functions, we will learn more about ourselves. Although mankind's greatest discoveries are often linked to chance events, the famous French chemist Louis Pasteur's famous phrase 'Fortune favours the prepared mind' applies perfectly to the chance appearance of the longed-for creative insights we all have, but we can prepare ourselves to have even more. Contemporary studies show that we solve as much as sixty percent of our problems without being able to explain in a logical, sequential way how we arrived at that solution. Knowing as much as possible about your car before you set off on holiday ensures you have a safer journey; so, let's get acquainted with our most valuable resource, our brain, and let's prepare it for the most important journey of all… Life.

Us and our brains

Our brain is, as far as we know, the most complex system in the entire universe. Thanks to some amazing technological advances in the study of the mind, it is believed that what physics, chemistry and microbiology were to the eighteenth, nineteenth and twentieth centuries, neuroscience will be to the twenty-first. Despite having learned more about the brain in the last ten years than in the entire history of humanity, there is still a great deal left to discover. What makes up our individuality as humans, our talent, our personality? Every intention, every dream, every action originates in the brain, which is designed to solve problems relating to survival in an unpredictable world in constant flux. And it does so simply as part of a survival strategy that allows us to pass on our genes to the next generation.

Overcoming the adversities of the environment throughout the history of the planet, in order to belong to the tiny group of privileged species that survives today, could be said to boil down to two factors: become stronger or more intelligent than the rest. That is to say, we either had to develop bigger muscles or more neurons in our brain. Human beings did the latter. And the neurons that started to accumulate in our prefrontal lobe (the last part of our actual brain to be formed) are what enabled us to separate from our closest cousin, the gorilla.

The researcher Judy DeLoache identified the specifically human ability to think symbolically or, as she referred to it, 'representational insight' – the capacity to attribute characteristics and meanings to objects which don't intrinsically possess them. In other words, we are able to invent things that don't exist;

we are humans because we can fantasise. When my daughter and I pretend that fallen twigs are airplanes that have landed on the ground, we are being *totally* human. The ability to combine symbols allows us to communicate through language, writing, art and mathematics. We can combine dots and squiggles to make music or poetry, we can combine circles and squares to produce Cubist paintings or geometry. We aren't born with this ability to detect and mentally represent the relation between a symbol and its referent (representational insight). In fact, we don't become completely functional in this type of reasoning until we are almost three years old, so that prior to that we aren't very different from monkeys. For example, if a two-and-a-half-year-old child playing with a doll's house places a miniature dog under the doll's bed and is told that in a similar, life-sized room next door there is another dog hidden, it won't occur to her to look under the bed when she enters the room. At three years old that would be the first place she looked. Thanks to this symbolic language, we are able to extract vast amounts of information and knowledge without the need for direct experience, which can be harsh. If, for example, I fall into a swamp and manage to get out, and I subsequently put up a sign saying 'Danger, swamp' or a picture of a swamp with a hand emerging from the surface, other people will avoid falling into it. It seems only logical that once we developed this tool that is our brain, we would preserve it.

To sum up: we continue to exist on this planet because we are more intelligent than any other living creature, and we owe our humanity in large part to the ability of our mind to fantasise. And although there is no doubting our creative potential, as with all other learning processes, it takes time to **evolve**. Thoughtful and applied practice of the techniques suggested in this book will help you to create more neural connections in your brain, which in turn will stimulate new and different thoughts.

Brain evolution

> 'You've got to learn your instrument. Then you
> practice, practice, practice. And then when you
> finally get up there on the bandstand, forget all that
> and just wail.'
>
> Charlie Parker

The first proto mammals (common ancestors to all mammals) existed approximately one hundred and eighty to two hundred million years ago. Thirty million years later, the first birds appeared. They shared the same challenges faced by reptiles and fish: a harsh environment and hungry predators. However, in proportion to their body size, both proto mammals and birds evolved large brains. Another important difference is that reptiles and fish do not nurture their young, some even eat them, and are solitary creatures. Mammals and birds, on the other hand, bring up their young and, in many cases, they form pairs, sometimes even mating for life. In neuroscience terms, selecting a good mate, sharing food and nurturing our young requires more complex neural processes: meaning that, from a scientific point of view, a squirrel or a parrot is more alive than a lizard or a salmon. They plan, communicate, cooperate and negotiate better. When human couples become parents, they discover that these abilities are essential, especially if they wish to stay together. The next evolutionary leap occurred eighty million years ago with the appearance of the primates. Monkeys and apes are characterised by their high levels of sociability and can spend up to a sixth of their day grooming one another. The more social success they enjoy, the more descendants they will have, and the more complex their social relationships, the more complex their brains. Tools are the strongest evidence to date indicating at what point we became human. If we look back through the history of our evolution, we could say that 2.6 million years ago we started scribbling on and breaking rocks; we made axes the size of the palm of our hand. Between then and now, the human brain has tripled in size. A million years later, we were still using the same stone axes, but we started to sharpen them by hitting them with other stones. Our first direct ancestor, the famous *Homo sapiens*, appeared about one hundred thousand years ago, and that was when our prefrontal lobe started to develop. Then something extraordinary occurred: forty thousand years ago, we started to make rock paintings, to sculpt and make jewellery. No one knows the reason for this sudden, rapid change, but most scientists attribute it to the natural pressure of the changing environment that boosted the impulse of the species to survive. It is thought that our first ancestors in eastern Africa consisted of a tribe of two thousand individuals. A hundred thousand years later, there are more than seven thousand million of us. Theories about why we have become so numerous, given the above-mentioned circumstances, suggest that rather than attempt to overcome the climate, we adapted to its variations. We didn't worry about having a constant habitat, because we knew that wasn't an option, and so instead of learning to survive in one or two places the way other species do, we conquered the entire planet. Those who were unable to solve the problem of the environment or learn swiftly from their mistakes wouldn't have survived long enough to pass on their genes, and the same applied to those who didn't cooperate with other clan members. The outcome of this evolution is that we didn't become stronger, but rather we became more intelligent! *And that was thanks to the changes in our brain.*

For a hundred thousand generations, since we invented the stone axe, genes favouring the ability to communicate and cooperate grew more prevalent in humans. We see the result today in altruism, generosity, our concerns about reputation, our justice systems, language, morality and religion. How it came about was through the interaction of two powerful aspects of the brain: on the one hand a memory, like a hard drive, which stores knowledge, and on the other our ability to improvise using that information.

I remember as a teenager taking saxophone lessons, and very quickly I wanted to start composing and improvising bossa nova melodies in the best tradition of Stan Getz. I had no idea that besides assimilating music theory and memorising scales and notes, I also needed to possess a deep understanding of that style of music. In order to be able to compose, I had to fill my hard drive with data and information. Similarly, in order to compose and improve my songs, I needed to be able to improvise on that database: use my creativity. Jazz musicians study for years to be able to master the rules, just so they can break them as quickly as possible. That capacity to improvise, to use our knowledge to be creative, is what allowed us to survive in a constantly changing environment. Today, more than ever, we need to use our very human capabilities to make a difference in society, in our work, in our education, so that we can enjoy a better life.

Use it or lose it

It is quite possible that each of us, unless we suffer from a specific medical condition, could run a twenty-six-mile marathon. In order to do so we must prepare, train, change our diet and be extremely disciplined. The same goes for that creative cerebral 'muscle' we all have; if we don't exercise it, it is very unlikely to develop.

As we saw, the moment we enter school, the world becomes increasingly logical and rational. We stop using our creative muscle the way we did when we were little, and our ability to do so starts to atrophy. If *we don't use, it we lose it*. Through various studies and different technologies, neuroscience has shown that this ability doesn't disappear altogether. And we can develop it at any age. It is thought, and many studies argue, that when we are being creative the activity in the right side of our brain is significantly increased; not only do the neural networks in that area of the brain participate in the creative process, they can also be exercised. But to achieve this we must make a conscious, sustained effort.

The left side of our brain processes information in a linear way, dealing with one thing at a time; it is also responsible for our ability to write, analyse, abstract, classify, use logic and rational thought, exercise judgement and verbal memory, use symbols and understand mathematics. The right side of our brain is able to assimilate a lot of information simultaneously; it gives us a holistic perspective and can detect similarities. It is the home of our intuition and the place where insights and revelations occur. Skilled at synthesising, visualising and recognising patterns and relating things to the present, it is also mainly responsible for our sensations. For example, the left side of the brain remembers names and the right side remembers faces. Reading a book about tennis is the job of the left side of the brain, but it is the right side that experiences the feeling of the ball engaging with the racket.

Both sides of the brain

Write down on a piece of paper the most desirable, extreme, sexy or apparently impossible-to-achieve ideas you can think of regarding your creative challenge.

Now write down on a second piece of paper all the most practical, logical down-to-earth ideas.

Look at both lists and try to connect them to see what comes out.

Stimulate the right side of the brain

Read a science fiction or fantasy novel

Scientific studies have proven that when we read a story that requires us to explore new meanings and use our imagination, we employ the right as well as the left side of our brain. Reading stories and novels exercises the intellectual skills necessary to think differently, more creatively. It offers us the possibility of exploring fresh meanings, obtaining a non-literal interpretation of what we read.

Be silent

Taking part in non-verbal activities decreases left-brain activity. That in turn reduces the activity of dominant thought patterns in the neural networks. It is like lowering the volume of our conscious mind.

Any activity or game that exercises our imagination

Brainteasers, board games, crosswords, improvised theatre or music, free-style dancing and many more related activities not only exercise our ability to generate multiple perspectives and ideas, they allow us to cultivate a fun attitude towards the creative process. When we are small, we are much more creative and we explore many more ideas. What better way to practise this approach than by becoming a child again?

Embrace ambiguity

Accepting it is crucial if we want to tap into multiple meanings, and it is something the right side of the brain loves doing. Ambiguity allows us to perceive an ocean of possibilities.

Professor John Kounios suggests that if you are working on a difficult problem, you should set your alarm a few minutes early so that you can doze in bed for a while. It's where we do some of our best thinking. Don't forget to write your thoughts down.

Squashed fried eggs

Falling in love, riding a bike, enjoying a view, the nagging toothache, the idea you had which you thought was amazing... they all begin with a neuron.

As with every organ, the brain is made up of different types of tissue, which in turn are composed of even smaller units called cells. All living organisms are made up of cells. If life is a great stage play, they are the part behind the scenes, supervising almost everything we experience. We could imagine a typical cell as a fried egg, the white being the cytoplasm and the yolk the nucleus. Inside it is like a big city where everything occurs at the level of a micron (a million times smaller than a metre): transport, hospitals, construction, communications, sanitation, hygiene, education and so on. Inside the nucleus we find the famous DNA, the bane nowadays of criminals and murderers. In our DNA are our genes, the building blocks containing the biological instructions that determine much of what we are, such as the colour of our eyes, or how sensitive we are to stressful situations. Incredibly efficient, in each nucleus is three yards of uniquely packaged DNA: imagine sixty miles of Internet cable inside a starburst.

Each cell in our body is morphologically different, according to its position and function. Nerve cells are also diverse and have different functions. The best known and most important of these as far as we are concerned are the neurons. If we step on a fried egg on the floor and it spatters over everything, we will obtain the shape that most resembles a neuron, a bit like a star with lots of prongs. If we place our finger on the prongs and pull, we will get the multi-toothed effect. That is a neuron. Basically it consists of a cell body (what is left of the squashed fried egg), the axon and the dendrites (the prongs and spikes of our star). The axon is electrically charged and extends from the body of the cell to its objective, for example another neuron or some muscle tissue. The dendrites receive messages from other neurons. Grey matter is what we call the sum of all the neuronal cell bodies, and white matter the axons and other cells known as glials. Glials have a supporting function, protecting the axons and recycling the brain's chemical messengers, the neurotransmitters. The most commonly known neurotransmitters are glutamate (which stimulates the neurons that receive information), GABA (which inhibits the neurons that receive information), serotonin (regulates the appetite by making us feel sated, controls sexual desire, body temperature, motor activity as well as perceptive and cognitive functions), dopamine (which is related to attention span and the reward system, promotes affective behaviour), norepinephrine (makes us attentive and stimulates us), acetylcholine (promotes learning and wakefulness), opioids (regulate stress, reduce pain and produce pleasure; they include the endorphin hormones), oxytocin (promotes nurturing, relationships and is associated with affection and love, women have more of it than men), vasopressin (promotes closeness between couples, in men it can lead to aggressive behaviour towards sexual rivals), cortisol (released by the adrenal glands as a response to stress), oestrogen (both the female and the male brain contain oestrogen receptors which affect libido, mood and memory).

The pathways in the brain are made up of approximately a hundred thousand million neurons. They are the foundations on which the nervous system is built. Their main function is to communicate among themselves through small links called synapses. These complex, electrically charged entities are designed to pass information to other neurons through nerves, muscles and various glands. Glands are tiny organs whose function is to synthesise chemical substances such as hormones, and release them, often into the bloodstream. Each neuronal signal is a fragment of information transmitted via the nervous system (in the same way blood flows through our blood vessels). All of this information is what we define as our mind in a broad sense. But be careful, because most of what occurs in the mind (some scientists suggest about eighty percent) is on an unconscious level, meaning we have no knowledge of it. The term 'mind' includes signals that control stress, our ability to ride a bike, our personality, and many more things. Our brain is dynamic and it shapes our mind. Brain and mind interact on such a profound level that they might be better understood as a single, interdependent system. It is a system which is so busy that, despite making up approximately two percent of our body weight, it uses twenty-five percent of the glucose and oxygen we consume – i.e. our energy. It works twenty-four hours a day, seven days a week, three hundred and sixty-five days a year, and consequently uses almost the same amount of energy regardless of whether we are asleep or deep in thought.

Contact

You fall in love with someone, to ride a bike you need a bicycle, you enjoy a sunset watching the brightest star drop below the horizon, your tooth aches because you have a cavity, you learned mathematics from seeing equations on a whiteboard, you had a great idea to solve a challenge at work. Even though everything begins with a neuron, it is the interactions between neurons, like our interactions with the world around us, that activates our reason, our emotions, OUR CREATIVITY, our instincts, our mind.

Synapses are the links enabling neurons to communicate. Imagine a row of neurons as a one-way street with a traffic light. If the signal being sent (through electrical impulses and the release of neurotransmitters) is to halt an activity, the traffic light will go red. If the signal is to initiate or continue an activity, the light will remain green until that information has reached its final destination – i.e. your foot kicking a ball. That signal can travel from two millimetres up to a metre. When an electrical impulse is triggered, the neuron undergoes a dramatic change, known as 'action potential', and the charge in the axon membrane switches from negative to positive. This occurs at a speed of a hundred miles per hour, and can fire off up to a thousand times a second. When the impulse finally reaches the extremity of the axon, that change in voltage triggers the release of neurotransmitters, which, on reaching their destination, attach to specialised receptors on the target cells. These receptors act like interrupters, switching on or off depending on which chemical is transmitted. Neurons contain tens of thousands of such connections, which can modify target cells. A neuron will typically fire off between five and fifty times a second. Neurons connect with other neurons, muscle or glands to form trillions of different patterns that reform, grow and migrate throughout our lifetime. This process of specification and migration begins in the embryo, roughly four weeks after conception. Genetic programming determines that the right type of neuron will be transmitted to a specific area, where the neuron's dendrites and axons will extend, connecting with other neurons. In this way the different structures in the brain will be formed, acquiring specific ways of transmitting messages and learning how to process and control our interactions with our environment, whether we are kicking a ball (motor function) or flying an airplane (complex memory).

Your mind will continue to learn and change until the day you die. This is due to the capacity of the brain itself to learn and change, also known as neuroplasticity. In general, when this occurs, the result is slight, incremental alterations in the neuronal structure that occur over the years. Your mind (thoughts) can change the structure and anatomy of your brain (in particular neurons).

We aren't destined biologically to become less creative as we grow older. Youthful innocence and optimism makes us more open to radical ideas, but if we continue to look for fresh challenges, we will still think like young people long after our hair turns grey.

Mental activity or thought can shape neural structures in a variety of ways. For instance, there is an increased blood flow to the busiest neural pathways, providing them with more glucose and oxygen; when neurons fire off simultaneously, the existing synapses are strengthened and new ones are formed in a process called neurogenesis; some pathways, which are rarely or never used, undergo a kind of neural pruning – a sort of survival of the most active. Neurons also grow in different areas of the brain, for example in the hippocampus, where neurogenesis increases memory pathways towards new learning. What's more, a growing number of studies suggest that positive emotional excitement aids learning by multiplying neural connections and strengthening synaptic change. This transformation in the structure of our brain goes beyond our subjective, momentary experience, creating lasting changes that affect our wellbeing, our ability to function and our relationships.

Recent scientific data show that we have good reason to treat ourselves well, to cultivate fulfilling experiences and to learn from them, because all our experiences will have a real, structural, anatomical impact on our brain, influencing and affecting our lives in the present as well as in the future.

Three brains

> 'The essential difference between emotion and
> reason is that emotion leads to action while reason
> to conclusions.'
>
> Donald Calne

Life on earth began around 3.5 thousand million years ago. The first multicellular organisms appeared around 650 million years ago. As animals evolved, so did their cells and neural tissues, which developed into the 'headquarters' we call the brain. *We have three brains coexisting inside us.* If we look at animal evolution, we can say in an extremely simplified way that before becoming primates we were simple mammals, and before that, reptiles. We still have a lizard-squirrel-monkey brain, which informs our responses. This is known as a 'triune brain' and is one of the models scientists use to describe the hierarchical organisation of our cerebral structures. It is like thinking about the construction of a house: first the foundations (reptile), then the walls (squirrel) and finally the roof (monkey), but they all form part of the same structure. The oldest part of the brain – the reptilian brain – is around five hundred million years old, and is largely in control of everything relating to the body's vital functions: breathing, the sleep-wake cycle, heart rate, and so on. The *squirrel* or limbic brain is about two hundred million years old and is in charge of everything relating to our survival rather than to our human potential: flight or fight in some extreme situations, feeding, reproducing. It contains a central part of our emotions: the amygdala (nothing to do with the ones in our throat), which enables us to feel anger, fear and pleasure. It is responsible for producing our emotions and the memories they generate. The limbic brain also houses the hippocampus, which converts memories from short to long term, and the thalamus, which acts like a control tower of the emotions. These two brains are oldest and they regulate our behaviour as people. Above them, like a cathedral, is our most human brain, the prefrontal cortex or primate brain, which appeared around a hundred thousand years ago. If we look at the age of these structures, it is like having lived in a house with no roof for millions of years.

The prefrontal cortex is highly specialised in vision, speech, memory and all decision-making functions. It is divided into two hemispheres, right and left, which are joined by the corpus callosum. As we evolved, the left hemisphere focused on processing information in a linguistic, linear way, and the right in a visual, holistic way. The two hemispheres work together, and many of the structures and neural regions are duplicated in each. Despite being on the surface, the prefrontal cortex is closely related to its inner core. It is the area folded in on itself giving the brain its wrinkles and grooves. If the prefrontal cortex hadn't folded, it would be the size of a small rug.

For many years, we thought we were 'rational beings (prefrontal cortex) with emotions (limbic brain)'. Today's scientists agree that the 'master switch' in our brain is the emotional region. *We are emotional beings who have learned how to think*, not thinking machines that feel. This makes sense if we consider that the limbic brain has been on the earth for over two hundred million years, and the prefrontal cortex scarcely a hundred thousand. Emotion holds far more sway over us than reason. Which is why many of the decisions we make in life are unconscious; the majority are determined by surges of emotion (some arising from memory, others from fresh emotions). Our rational mind will often justify decisions we made before we realised we had made them. In short: the cerebral control that governs our behaviour when we are confronted with different everyday situations is more influenced by our emotions than by reason. If you can learn to free your unconscious mind, it will help release more creative ideas and better solutions.

Common creative blocks

The following are questions about the most common types of problems or challenges we encounter in our work, and are aimed at providing opportunities for you to generate ideas and solve them creatively:

▲ What do you want to obtain from your work, or to achieve in it?

▲ What topic or idea would you like to be working on?

▲ What do you want to happen in your work?

▲ Which work relationships would you like to improve upon?

▲ What are your unfulfilled aims?

▲ What part of your work do you love and find exciting?

▲ What part annoys and concerns you?

▲ What would you like others to do?

▲ What changes would you like to introduce?

▲ Where are the bottlenecks?

▲ What aspect of your work would you like to organise better?

The following are typical challenges in the work environment that enable you to use your creativity:

▲ What creative suggestions can I make to generate new products?

▲ How can we cut costs in order to increase production?

▲ How can we differentiate our products from those of our competitors?

▲ What changes to existing products are needed?

Continued

- How can I increase my sales by twenty percent?
- How can I make myself indispensable to my company?
- How can I inspire my employees or my colleagues to search actively for ways of differentiating us from our competitors?
- What would employees like to be rewarded for?
- How can we change our image?
- How can we triumph over our competitors?

Lights, camera, action... brain!

'Think in the morning.
Act in the noon.
Eat in the evening.
Sleep in the night.'

William Blake

As we have already seen, during our evolution we managed to survive on the planet because we became more intelligent. This was thanks to our prefrontal cortex. Greater intelligence meant an increasingly bigger prefrontal cortex, with a greater number of connections. Our head had to grow to accommodate it; let's remember that if the prefrontal cortex hadn't folded in on itself, it would be the size of a baby blanket by now. Imagine the enormous hips a woman would have needed to give birth to an infant with a head like that, not to mention the impossibility of being able to run fast enough to escape the dangers of that

African era. And so, in its wisdom, natural selection came up with an evolutionary anatomical compromise which solved the problem: a smaller head that can pass through the birth canal, and contains a larger brain folded in on itself. Exactly as our brain is today.

Childhood was also invented during that evolutionary period. Human babies have to complete their development outside the womb. Newborns are vulnerable to predators and don't become fertile for more than a decade.

We are born with a small head that can pass through our mother's pelvis, but it is a long time before we are able to confront the world alone, independently. Our great-great-great-grandparents depended on their mothers, who needed the fathers to provide food. We all need cooperation and teamwork to function in complex social groups. Such social structures contributed to the brain's continued growth in size and complexity, developing empathy, disappointment, altruism and building alliances.

Our new brain separates us from all other creatures on earth, endowing us with extraordinary capabilities such as linear thinking, the elaboration of complex language, the ability to interpret signs and symbols, to develop and understand mathematical strategies, to communicate eloquently and meaningfully. Traditions, concepts, patterns, ideas, folklore and customs came into being and were passed down the generations. Eventually, small groups started to migrate, to explore and to readapt.

In addition, during that age of extreme vulnerability, babies were ready to learn, although they couldn't do much. Not only did the concept of *learning* arise but that of the *teacher* too. It was in our interests as a species to be excellent teachers, because our survival depended on how well we educated and protected our offspring. There was little point in raising children only for them to be devoured by our neighbours the leopards. It was during this evolutionary period when the final part of the prefrontal cortex or frontal lobe (located beneath the forehead), evolved. This region of the brain gave us more dexterity so that we could create pointed spears, as well as enabling us to *socialise* with other members of the clan: we needn't develop more muscle in order to overcome a mammoth or a leopard, but we could obtain the same result through teamwork. Our dominance over the planet was beginning, and the rules of the game were about to change. We learned to cooperate, which meant having shared objectives that took account of our own interests as well as those of our allies. And for that we needed to be able to understand what motivated others, including their systems of reward and punishment.

Thanks to the prefrontal cortex, we became better hunters and are still here today. The reason why this new region of the brain is of such interest to us now, is because it is the part we use most in our day-to-day work. It is the central area of the brain where we 'think' about stuff, where all our conscious interactions with the world connect. We use it whenever we generate thoughts; some people call it 'working memory'. The prefrontal lobe is the region of the brain that consumes most energy because it is responsible for understanding, making decisions, memorising, remembering and suppressing certain thoughts, to enable us to work or achieve something that requires all our attention and awareness. Imagine the brain containing a full tank of fuel (largely made up of glucose and oxygen) necessary for it to carry out all its functions. The prefrontal cortex uses most of this valuable fuel; no matter how hard we try, the nature of thought is fleeting. This is a biological limitation. Some scientists affirm that because the prefrontal cortex is such a new region of the brain, it still hasn't evolved and developed enough to be energy efficient. We should understand that if we carry out activities involving the prefrontal cortex, after a few hours we are going to feel exhausted and unable to think clearly.

The Theory of Mind

The Theory of Mind is an expression used to describe our capacity to attribute thoughts and intentions to others, not unlike the ability to 'read' people's minds and predict what the matter is or what they want. This requires a tremendous amount of mental activity. Many scientists argue that our intellectual supremacy over the planet is directly related to the development of this ability. When we predict another person's state of mind, we are detecting signals that are by no means obvious. We do this automatically; often without realising we are doing it. The Theory of Mind gives rise to the notion that our capacity to learn is closely linked to the way in which we relate to others. Efficiency in learning is related to the emotional atmosphere in which learning takes place. Many studies show the importance of the pupil–teacher relationship in correct learning. We could extend this concept to other relationships: boss–employee, father–son and so on.

In short, reason and logic (prefrontal cortex) make us human and differentiate us from other animals. However, as beings we are still more emotional than rational. So, reason vs. emotion? Not really. We are the result of a remarkable interaction between the two.

The past: present and correct?

In his book, *The Buying Brain*, Dr A. K. Pradeep recounts four clever stories illustrating the differences, or rather the similarities, between the intellectual life of our early ancestors a hundred thousand years ago in Africa, and our life today.

Let's travel back in time to see what life was like a hundred thousand years ago. . .

You wake up on the African plain on a parched day, the sun on your face. You are hungry and cold. Your brain, geared towards fulfilling aims (your new prefrontal cortex commands your body fulfil its most pressing needs), compels you to go in search of food. You seize your spear, also relatively new, and leave your refuge. Your anxiety levels increase; your senses are heightened, your ears monitor every sound in a three hundred and sixty degree circle. Your eyes scan the horizon, your nose tries to detect the scent of other animals, water, plants. Your mouth is dry and your muscles are tense and prepared. Your breathing is rapid and your heartbeat is accelerated. After two hours, your eyes, ears and nose alert you to something moving in the long grass. Suddenly a tail appears, and you see the flashing eyes of a leopard. With incredible speed your brain calculates the next step. The leopard can outrun you. Should you flee? But your spear is lethal and you are hungry. Should you fight? Instantly you make a decision. The leopard is also hungry, and its intentions are obvious as it slinks towards you baring its fangs. Its whiskers twitch as it enters a state of maximum alert. It takes the decision and pounces. You are two dangerous predators who are both very hungry. Only one of you will survive. Your heart is beating fast, your body perspires and your muscles quiver as you confront this life-or-death situation. The fight is short but bloody. You are wounded, but you will return to the refuge with your spear. The leopard is immobilised and your body is secreting endorphins – the 'I feel good' hormone that gives you a sense of euphoria. You carry the leopard on your back and walk the few miles to your home, scaring away crows and hyenas that want to steal your quarry. Your fellow tribe members welcome you joyfully; they prepare a feast and clean your wounds. Now the reward system in your brain is activated, and the sense of pride and duty fulfilled takes deep root in your psyche. This will impel you to go out hunting another day.

When the brain's behaviour–reward system is activated, it releases large amounts of dopamine that stimulate us to try again and to repeat what we have just done. For a while, this system of repetitive behaviour activates our reward pathways and other neurological systems that encourage us to improve our performance and to do it more effortlessly and frequently.

Physically and emotionally drained, you fall into a replenishing sleep. A new day dawns.

The same brain today, twenty-first century...

You wake up to the sound of your digital alarm clock. You are warm and snug. Instead of focusing on the search for food to ensure your survival, you examine your fridge to see what 'low-calorie' option you should eat. The need to find food is seldom, if ever, one of the main motivators that spurs you into action. And yet, your primitive brain still feels the urge to hunt, to achieve, and so the day's mission assumes the status of a life-or-death scenario. You check your email and notice that one of your suppliers has sent you an attachment. Just as on the hungry African plain, your anxiety increases; you become tense and on high alert. Your brain compels you to find some relief. You grab your mobile phone and your laptop and drive to work. As you sit in traffic, your brain feels under threat. Car horns beep in unison and your amygdala (the part of your brain that responds to stress) starts to ignite. Your blood pressure rises and your heart beats faster. Endless advertisements along the road entice and assault you. You turn on the radio. The stock market has plummeted. Your feeling of security is once again threatened. Your irritation peaks when a car tries to overtake where it shouldn't. Enraged, you prevent it with a manoeuvre worthy of a racing driver. You arrive at work and park your car. In the car park, a group of sweaty, shaking youths try to steal your laptop, your mobile phone and your money. Your survival instinct kicks in. You shout and try to elbow your way through them. Confronted by you, they are now as angry as they are desperate; no longer content with your laptop, they want your life. Your heart starts thumping as your muscles begin to quiver. Just in time, two security guards arrive, and the youths flee. You collapse with relief. Hours, days and weeks later, your brain will continue to relive the scene from beginning to end. You will dream about it every night. Your fear threshold is now lower, and your security feels under constant threat. Your level of cortisol (the stress hormone) has increased, improving your alertness and performance.

And yet, you don't go into fight or flight mode the way you did a hundred thousand years ago, but instead you enter your office and sit down at your desk. You interact with your colleagues all day, attempting to influence and outmanoeuvre them.

> Your level of cortisol (the stress hormone) increases, improving your alertness and performance.

You are 'on your game', allying with those who support your aims and contemplating those who could destroy you. You are completely focused on that. It is dark by the time you drive home, and hundreds of flickering lights accompany you on your way. Your brain struggles to try to decipher all the messages those lights are firing at you. Most of them are irrelevant. Any messages that are new or significant will register in your hippocampus and be stored more permanently in your prefrontal cortex. You arrive home, switch on one or all of your three screens, and spend hours receiving, sending or checking other messages (texts, emails, Internet, adverts etc.) You fall into a sleep that isn't the replenishing one necessary for your memory to store the information that could help you to adapt better the next day.

Now let's travel back once more a hundred thousand years, only this time we will compare a day in the life of a woman then and now...

You wake up perspiring with a hungry baby in your arms. You clean it and feed it and then go in search of food for yourself. You are dangerously thin and very thirsty. Your baby needs to suckle from you, using all your reserves of fat. With your baby on your back, you venture a few yards from your refuge. The other women, adolescents and children from the tribe go with you. You approach a place where a few days before you found some delicious berries and roots. When the children fall asleep, some of the women guard them while the others continue to forage for berries, seeds, roots and an occasional rodent or snake. The women stay close together, constantly on the alert for predators, ready to stand up to the wild animals to protect their young. And yet, they would never attack a large, dangerous predator. Their prefrontal cortex knows that a 'win-or-lose' attack would leave their children defenceless, possibly dead. Without them knowing it, this restraint allows them to achieve their aim in the evolution of the species: to procreate successfully.

The group of women and children spend the day together collecting food and supporting one another. However, if one of them resorts to lies or deception, it might give them and their progeny an evolutionary advantage. It is the women's task to look after the sick and they quickly learn to interpret the needs and desires of others, especially those of their own offspring, who can only communicate through facial expressions and eye contact. Without the need for spoken language, the women know if they are crying from hunger, irritation, boredom or anxiety. The female brain has therefore evolved a capacity for empathy, and women can often understand others' needs or desires simply by looking at them.

As the women look after their children all day, their bodies are awash with oxytocin, making them calm, even slightly sedated, though completely committed to their task.

When night falls, the men return. Some have caught large prey that will provide the whole tribe with the protein and calories it needs. The women celebrate the catch and reward the successful hunter (prowess beats good looks), while responding timidly and cautiously towards the men who have come back empty-handed, in order not to increase their frustration. The women will then choose the most successful hunters and procreate with them. After they have eaten, and as they listen to the hunters' tales (related in grunts), the women lie down beside their men cradling their babies.

The same brain, a hundred thousand years later...

You turn off your alarm clock, shower and hurriedly get dressed. It is still dark outside, so you have plenty of time to get through your long to-do list. You prepare your children's schoolbags and their packed lunches. You look at the calendar to see what activities they have today. You sign a permission note for an excursion and leave a note for the childminder telling her that your daughter has a dental appointment that afternoon and that your son is playing football. You check the fridge and make a note of what needs buying and what your kids can eat after school. You pay the bills online before you wake them up, help them dress and give them breakfast. You grab your laptop and your mobile phone and set off. You are already in the car when your daughter decides she doesn't like the dress you have chosen for her and starts to cry. But you quickly employ your empathic skills to save the situation. Suddenly you remember that it's your turn to do the school run and you have to turn round. Exasperated, you arrive late at the other kids' houses and have to put up with their parents' annoyance. You take the main road, and it is a free-for-all. Aggressive drivers slam on their brakes, lean on their horns and overtake when they shouldn't. Your brain experiences this as a 'life-and-death' situation. Your heart starts to beat faster, you become increasingly anxious and cortisol floods your system. And yet your brain is prepared to cope with imminent dangers and possible assaults. You race to work, arriving late for a meeting and almost out of breath. While you are giving a presentation to your colleagues, part of your brain is still thinking about your kids. Did you remember to put fruit in their packed lunch? Was that sniffle the early sign of a cold, or an allergy? You immerse yourself in your work, filling in budget spreadsheets and completing orders. Your multitasking brain connects easily to both hemispheres. You skip lunch because you are behind. At two-thirty, the childminder calls. Your daughter is sick. Now your brain gives out alarm signals left, right and centre! Your priority is to protect your children. You grab your things and leave in a hurry, even though your brain tells you that what your boss or colleagues say might threaten your career. You drive fast, constantly checking the time. You are going to be later than you said you would be and your breathing becomes quick and shallow. Every red light exasperates you. Come on! Come on! Hurry up! Hurry up! You arrive fifteen minutes late and your kids are irritable and sulky. You drop one daughter off at the doctor and your son at the football pitch, and then you go back to the doctor. You didn't have time to watch your son warming up, or sit with your daughter at the doctor. And yet your brain enjoys the contentment of having them near. You go home, it's seven in the evening and the fridge is bare. You've been up for more than twelve hours and you still haven't managed to spend fifteen minutes of quality time with your kids. You help them with their homework, order a takeaway pizza and switch on your computer in order to finish the work you couldn't do earlier. After a supper lasting twenty minutes, the children go to their rooms and then to bed. You feel a bit uneasy because you haven't been able to talk to your kids, your partner or your friends all day. At ten o'clock, after checking over your work, your partner arrives just as you are taking the clothes out of the washing machine. You talk for a while and then finally, at around midnight, you go to bed, exhausted. Your dreams are filled with symbolic threats and attacks as your brain attempts to process what has happened during the day.

Your brain has evolved to be able to multitask, the way your ancestors did when they looked after the children while foraging for food and attending to the sick.

Women are experts at being efficient; the female brain has more connections between the right and left hemispheres than in the average male brain. This makes it easier for women to juggle emotions, logic and the many different daily tasks they have to perform.

Compared to their ancestors, many women today have many more responsibilities. The ability to keep their nearest and dearest close to them is constantly under threat from the prevailing lifestyle in the modern metropolis.

These stories clearly show us how emotion and instinct are the true drivers of human behaviour, whether thousands of years ago or today, in the twenty-first century.

In the next chapter, we will start to delve into the world of creativity.

THE CREATIVE PROCESS

Tradition is not for everyone

'Trust uncertainty, to bring you to clarity.'

Joanna Swanger

There are five main stages in the creative process. The first is *preparation*. We immerse ourselves, consciously or unconsciously, in a series of dilemmas or challenges that interest us or arouse our curiosity. What do I want to solve? What interests me? This is what we call the creative challenge. Occasionally we might make a creative discovery without much preparation.

The second stage is *incubation*. An idea ferments in our unconscious, combining to create new connections, without us consciously guiding it along narrow, linear pathways. We 'sleep on it'. Part of this process is conscious, although the incubation stage is often considered the most creative precisely because it occurs largely in the unconscious. Conscious thought can be analysed using logic and reason, but what happens in the dark, empty spaces defies analysis, and gives rise to the mystery surrounding creativity. Some even speak of creativity in mystical terms, the inspirational muse. Incubation can take minutes, hours or years.

The third stage is *insight*. Archimedes' famous 'eureka' moment, when the final piece of the puzzle slots into place. Insights can occur at any moment, and when they do we remember them with great intensity and excitement. They often arise after prolonged periods of work, rather like a cork bobbing to the surface when you hold it underwater and then let go. Experience tells us that important or creative insights arise when our minds are prepared, often after reflecting or working at length on a specific problem, challenge or subject. But there are also situations where creative ideas occur without anyone having posed a question and where no problem has been identified – i.e. when someone discovers both the problem and the solution. Later on, we will see what happens to the brain just before and during an insight.

The fourth stage is *evaluation*. Here, we must decide whether our insight has any value. This is an extremely sensitive moment, when we must process the idea and decide whether to pursue it or not, and we are frequently plagued with insecurities or doubts, because we are in the realm of the unknown. This is also where the criticisms begin, our own or those of others. Our colleagues with their opinions and prejudices… It's like when you paint a picture and stand back to see the overall effect, when you re-read something you have written, when scientists go over their calculations or equations to make sure they add up. Most insights don't get past the evaluation stage, but when they feel right, when they truly make sense, then we begin the work of elaboration, the longest and most arduous stage of the process. This is Edison's 'ninety-nine percent perspiration and one percent inspiration'. When we have an insight we think might help to solve our creative challenge, the process rarely ends there. Now the real work begins: we must apply our idea, modify it, be courageous, and convince others, all of which can sometimes mean leaving our comfort zone. Reality shows us that our new idea needs polishing. *The sketches our right brain makes have to become works of art.* This isn't necessarily the most fun part of the task, but it is essential.

These five stages are meant as a rough guideline. Many people contribute creatively in their field or in their own lives without having to go through each stage. The process isn't always linear, and there will be lots of twists and turns where more insights will be needed. A lot also depends on the depth or urgency of our creative challenge, or the problem we want to solve.

The five stages of creativity are a simplified model of what is otherwise a complex process, and occasionally might seem confusing. The important thing to remember is that they aren't absolute; they frequently overlap and occur continually throughout the process before it is complete. Don't think too much, synthesise.

Some amusing questions

Making your problem into an imaginary person can help you understand it, and also make it less daunting. If your problem were a living being, what would he or she look like? Draw your problem in the form of a living being. Imagine past and future reincarnations of your problem. Imagine you could eat your problem.

What would it taste like?

Is there something especially beautiful about your problem?

Is there something especially interesting about your problem?

Can you imagine your problem's private life?

What does it think about politics and tradition?

What kind of love life would it have?

When was it born? Does it have brothers or sisters? Does it have friends? Does it have fears?

If you were your problem's shrink or therapist, what would it talk to you about?

How do we get ideas?

Did you know that one of the things that uses up the most energy in our brain is thinking new thoughts? Which also explains why it is so difficult.

Creativity feeds on ideas, which originate somewhere. Ideas are created in our brain, our mind. One of the most interesting studies explaining how ideas arise is Eric Kandel's 'Cognitive Neuroscience and the Study of Memory', which earned him a Nobel Prize for Physiology and Medicine in 2000. Kandel and his fellow researchers have come up with a new concept of the brain known as 'intelligent memory'. Most neuroscientists have now rejected Dr Roger Sperry's theory of the right and left hemispheres. According to Kandel's theory, there is no such thing as the left and right brain, only analysis and intuition working simultaneously in every type of thought pattern: learning and memory combining in different ways throughout the brain.

In simple terms, Kandel's theory tells us that our experiences from the moment we are born, including everything that we learn, read, see or are told, is recorded somewhere in our brain. The image I like to use to understand Kandel's theory is that of a brain full of drawers: everything we experience, everything we learn is stored in one of those drawers, in our 'intelligent memory'; the brain as a gigantic chest of drawers.

The drawers start to open and close, and the memories inside them connect randomly. And the more relaxed we are, the more they open and close and the more connections they make. When that happens at some point during the day or night, we have 'more' ideas than at other times. When and where those moments of mental clarity occur depends a lot on the individual: we might be taking a shower, jogging, driving, on an underground train or bus, or in the park pushing our daughter on a swing.

When the brain is more relaxed, it generates more ideas. Some of these will be unexceptional or trivial, but others will be what we could call creative. The more ideas we have, the more chance there is one of them will be creative. In short: ideas are random combinations of concepts, experiences, patterns, thoughts and anecdotes stored in our intelligent memory, in the drawers in our brain. 'Novelty' arises from the different ways in which we combine what we already know. Suddenly, those combinations colliding with one another appear in our consciousness. We 'see' the idea. We have had an insight. The more mental clarity we have, the more likely we are to experience insights. The less noisy our unconscious, the more relaxed we are, enjoying doing something we really like, the more insights we will have.

> Beethoven would try out seventy different versions of a musical phrase before deciding on one. 'I make lots of changes, I discard them and try again, until I'm satisfied,' he once told a friend. It is totally normal to keep refining your ideas until you hit on the one that seems right to you.

Some of the world's most innovative companies understand this extremely well. They give their employees time off in flexible, spacious, luminous areas where they are free to imagine the future. They know that in a relaxed environment, removed from stress and the daily routine, their employees will generate more ideas. And, as we have already seen, statistically speaking, the more ideas we have, the greater the chance one of them will be creative; if an organisation is generous towards its employees, they in turn will be generous towards the organisation. When Lionel Messi plays for Argentina, he is exactly the same person with the same brain as when he plays for Barcelona. And yet when he plays for Barça, he will get on the ball ten or fifteen times and score at least two or three goals. Compared to two or three times when he plays for Argentina; resulting in fewer goals and less-inspired playing. The level of his game and the way he uses his skill and creativity depends a lot on his surroundings, the atmosphere during training, his teammates, his manager, how comfortable he feels. Creativity isn't a magic button that can be switched on anywhere. It is closely linked to our environment. In order to be creative we need a stimulating atmosphere.

Abstract drawing technique

Draw some abstract shapes, anything that comes into your head. Draw quickly, instinctively.

Choose one of your drawings. The one that most appeals to you or catches your eye. Let your instinct decide.

Identify its basic characteristics. For example, soft, fluffy, solid, strange, round, angular, etc.

Use it to inspire another drawing with a different shape.

Think about what that shape reminds you of (a cloud, a cat, a yoghurt pot, a soldier, a flag, etc.)

Associate the concepts you have discovered in your drawing with your creative challenge.

One thing is for sure: we all have insights during the day or night. However, up-to-date studies show that we forget very quickly most of the ideas arising from this association of concepts – this opening and closing of drawers. So, never underestimate the power of an idea that 'comes from nowhere' at the most inopportune moment. Make a note of it immediately, either on a piece of paper or one of your touchscreen devices. Write it down. Reread your notes. Erase any that are irrelevant so they don't clutter up your field of vision.

Try to remember your last ten good ideas. Where were you when you had them? Write them down. Write everything down.

First of all, produce

'Ideas are like rabbits. You get a couple and pretty soon you have a dozen.'

John Steinbeck

'If you want to have good ideas you must have many ideas. Most of them will be wrong and what you have to learn is which ones to throw away.'

Linus Pauling

We have talked about productive thinking, the friend of creativity, how we go about generating fresh thoughts – as opposed to reproductive thinking, which is usually the repetition of what we already know. But we can also discuss how much we produce, generating lots of ideas; lots of passes ending in a goal.

When Edison perfected the electric light bulb and invented the battery, an assistant asked him how he managed to keep on trying to make his inventions work after so many failures. Edison replied that he didn't understand the question: these weren't failures, he had simply discovered ways in which his inventions didn't work.

During his lifetime, Picasso produced an astonishing fifty thousand paintings, sculptures and drawings. Obviously, not everything in this vast body of work has been exhibited. Picasso understood that to create something different, something the public appreciated, first of all he needed to produce a lot. We must produce and generate lots of ideas before concentrating on one that we think is better, or different from the rest. And to do so we must abandon ourselves, allow our thoughts to flow freely, without criticism or judgement, which are counterproductive and inhibit creativity. We find this difficult because we are educated and conditioned to be critical and we are constantly making judgements. We judge new ideas and thoughts in an instantaneous, instinctive way; a bit like driving with one foot on the brake and the other on the accelerator. Consequently, we are apt to spend too much time – for example, during a brainstorming session – imagining all the reasons why an idea won't work or can't be implemented, instead of focusing on generating as many new ideas as possible. The moment we or someone else judges an idea, creative thought is blocked. When this happens, the few fresh ideas that emerge will soon slip back into the old, conservative thought patterns in our brains. Thinking without judging is a fluid, dynamic process, in which ideas soon begin to bounce off one another, producing fresh combinations, fresh associations, sparking an endless flow of creative possibilities.

'There's a way to do it better – find it.'

Thomas Edison

The SCAMPER technique

SCAMPER is a brainstorming technique for beginners, or for people who don't know how to debate issues in a logical way. It works by posing a series of appropriate, calculated questions. The questions are related to the words Substitute, Combine, Adapt, Modify, Put to other uses, Eliminate, Rearrange (or Reverse).

For example, if my aim is to 'improve my team's productivity', I begin with the letter 'S' from substitute: I can substitute people, places, procedures. What do I do? Change my team? Fire people? Hire others? Switch jobs? Change the way I implement projects? Change team leader? Change offices or meeting rooms?

The 'C' in Scamper stands for combine. I combine topics, concepts and ideas. Do I combine jobs? Do I put my best salespeople behind a desk and send the worst ones out to sell to see what happens? Do I combine their work with some leisure activity?

The 'A' stands for adapt. I adapt ideas taken from other contexts. And so on...

You will end up generating answers to all those hypothetical questions, many of which will be new ideas, or old ones you have modified, which you will evaluate and which will be useful in your creative challenge.

Another obstacle to creativity can be when a good idea prevents us from coming up with an even better one. That's why we have to give ourselves time to generate ideas, without worrying whether they are any good or not, whether they are feasible or if they solve the problem. As a way of focusing energy, I suggest taking the time/quantity challenge, a strategy which innovative companies often use: try to generate a hundred ideas in an hour.

Think of, and write down, a hundred different uses a brick can have. The first twenty or so will be the obvious ones we all think of: to build a wall, to make steps, to construct a barbecue, to hold up bookshelves, etc. The next thirty, forty or fifty ideas will start to become a bit more original, and as you get closer to the one hundred mark, your mind will make an extra effort to generate alternatives which are much more creative or imaginative. In order to perform this task efficiently, it is essential we curb our inner critic and start jotting down all our ideas, even the obvious ones or those we think are bad. The first thirty or so will include all the habitual uses; the next thirty will be more interesting, and the last thirty will doubtless reveal fresh insights, interests and complexities. Clearly, if we hadn't been forced to generate so many ideas, we would never have come up with the last thirty.

Creative thinking depends a lot on that constant generating of ideas, which eventually enables us to discard the most obvious ones, allowing the more unusual or imaginative ones to arise.

An excellent way to generate lots of ideas during the week is to write them down the moment they arise, listing them under headings in a notebook or on a mobile phone. As we have already seen, ideas appear and disappear in a flash. Aside from that hour we spend generating ideas, our brain is working around the clock, and insights can occur at any time, more so during moments of mental clarity. Building a library of our ideas enables us to think more quickly and to focus our attention. It is a simple, powerful strategy, and also quite a surprising one, because it uses our compulsive side, and also helps us to become more fluid, flexible thinkers. The more we write things down, the quicker, more malleable our thinking becomes.

Mental fluidity

In order to think more fluidly (quantity) and more flexibly (creativity), make lists.

Making lists is a powerful way to enhance the fluidity of your thinking.

For example, spend a few minutes listing all the possible uses a bicycle might have. Although you will generate lots of ideas, you will also censor some of them, and only write down the more obvious ones. In order to break away from that self-censorship, you need to be flexible. Allow yourself to write down lots of alternative ideas.

Flexibility of thought means being able to see beyond the commonplace and conventional. It means allowing thought to improvise more.

An exercise to stimulate fluid, flexible thinking

Write down a four-word sentence ('I like eating peaches').

Write down some more four-word sentences, starting with the first letter of each word in the first sentence.

For example: 'is love energy-producing' or 'ingenious lizards evade predators'.

Impasses and insights

'An insight is like finding a needle in a haystack.
There are a trillion possible connections in the brain,
and we have to find the exact one we need.'

Mark Beeman

Think of your creative potential as a raging forest fire. Fierce, blazing energy, spreading and growing with explosive force. Forest fires don't come magically from nowhere. Like creativity, they begin with a spark. One of the biggest blocks to creativity is the idea that we have to think up and elaborate the perfect solution before starting to work on our creative challenge. Every creative project I have worked on began life as a simple yet perfect spark of inspiration. And every creative challenge undergoes several transformations and changes of direction before reaching its final resolution.

Creative blocks are referred to in neuroscience as impasses. They occur when you are using your conscious mind to try to solve a problem, and you reach a dead end. An impasse is like a boulder blocking the path of your mental volition, a connection you want to make but which you can't pin down: you want to remember the name of an old acquaintance, to think about what to call your newborn baby, or perhaps your mind goes blank when you are trying to write about a project. Everyone experiences blocks or impasses all the time. When we need to be creative, it is essential to find a way of avoiding or getting round them.

Studies show that in today's world, more than half of all employees perform tasks that involve some element of creativity: describing, inventing, designing, drawing, colouring, re-contextualising, etc. Essentially creating or transmitting information in a new way. Innovation is a powerful magnet that can attract large profits, which demonstrates that the creative process is an important driving force generating value for companies. Although much of our working day is spent performing routine tasks that don't require much creativity, we often encounter unfamiliar problems for which there are no procedures or obvious explanations, and which call for fresh solutions.

The most effective way to overcome impasses and enable insights to arise is to silence the activity of the prefrontal cortex where conscious thought is generated. It is the noisy cortex that causes impasses. Today's technology allows us to measure what happens in our brain when we tackle different problems. Dr Mark Beeman, from Northwestern University, observed that forty percent of the time we try to solve problems in a logical way, testing one idea after another until something clicks. The other sixty percent of the time we do so by means of 'insights', which are characterised by a lack of any logical progression towards a solution, and often arise suddenly and unexpectedly. As we already saw when looking at the creative process, the unconscious plays an important part in the formation of insights, which can arise at odd times and places, often when our brain isn't engaged in a conscious effort to solve a problem, but is doing something different.

I already mentioned that when confronted with a fresh problem, we frequently resort to strategies that have worked in the past. Providing the new problem is similar to the old one and doesn't require fresh, creative solutions this may work. However, trying to address new problems with old solutions is the wrong strategy. It prevents better solutions from appearing and causes impasses. What science shows us is that we often become trapped in an impasse because the wrong answers are blocking the right ones. Getting out of an impasse is like trying to control a one-way flow of traffic over a bridge; you have to stop the cars on one side from driving onto the bridge to enable those on the other side to drive over it. When you take a break from a problem, your active, conscious thoughts diminish, allowing your unconscious to start speaking to you. That's why other people often find the answers to your problem. They aren't trapped in your way of thinking, and can see things from a different angle. When you find yourself in an impasse, don't try to focus more intensely on the problem (which increases your anxiety), instead take a few moments to do something different, something fun or interesting. This may seem counterintuitive, but it's the best way to stimulate fresh insights.

Beeman observed that people who solve problems by means of insights show increased activity in the right anterior temporal lobe, located just below the right ear. It forms part of the right hemisphere, and is the area most related to holistic thinking and gathering information from disparate regions of the brain. This is reminiscent of those drawers that open and close, brimming with ideas that combine to create fresh concepts in our right anterior temporal lobe. Other observations show that during the split second before an insight occurs, the brain appears to be extremely calm. During that moment, there is a sudden, prolonged burst of electrical, so-called alpha wave activity in the right occipital lobe, the area responsible for processing visual information. This alpha activity subsides at the precise moment when the insight occurs. It's as if, just before solving the problem, the brain switches off everything relating to visual function, silencing the interference caused by visual stimulus to allow the brain to find a solution: 'Be quiet, I'm trying to think!'

We all know what it's like talking to someone when suddenly their eyes start to wander and they look distracted. In fact, it's their brain reducing visual input in order to focus on the subtle, internal signals that precede an insight. It seems we need to do this in order for the insight to arise.

Solitary brainstorming exercise

Write down a few ideas on some index cards. One idea per card.

As you do so, put each card aside.

Write down your ideas as they occur to you, no matter if they are good, bad, weird, wonderful, or all those things. They don't need to be logical or useful.

The aim is to generate as many ideas as you can, and not to evaluate them until you have finished writing them all down.

When you have done that, gather up the cards and start separating and evaluating them.

How?

Combine the ideas you have written down and generate others through free association, imagine how an idea might work and then change it, turn it on its head to see if the opposite of what you wrote might work better, rearrange it, substitute it for similar ideas, consider each idea from different angles, draw a diagram or a picture of them, create metaphors for them, try to make connections between two or more ideas, imagine ways in which your idea might be criticised and try to adapt it accordingly, and, above all, go to bed and let your brain work on its own.

At the precise moment when an insight arises, gamma brainwaves appear. This happens thirty milliseconds before the answer appears in our consciousness. Gamma brainwaves are the highest frequency brainwave, and represent a group of neurons that fire off together, simultaneously. Gamma frequency activity occurs when different parts of the brain start communicating with one another. Relating this to Kandel's theory, imagine drawers opening and closing in different areas of your brain, connecting apparently unrelated concepts to form a new idea or insight. People who practise deep meditation produce high levels of gamma brainwaves, while those with learning difficulties produce low levels, and someone who is unconscious or in a coma produces none. Insights are also accompanied by a powerful surge of energy, which you can see in people's face, voice and body language. It feels good, almost euphoric. It is during this short-lived energy peak that we are at our most focused and have the courage to act. But once that cocktail of neurochemicals vanishes, our motivation quickly subsides. So, we have to move, act as quickly as possible after an insight occurs.

Let go

When a monkey sees a container of nuts, he goes over to it, sticks his hand inside and grabs some. But the neck of the container is too narrow for him to pull his hand out unless he lets go of the nuts. But the monkey doesn't want to do that, and so he gets stuck. We get stuck, too, when we won't let go of our opinions, concerns, beliefs and anxieties.

Exercise for getting rid of a mental block

Imagine that what is blocking you is physically embodied in something you are wearing: a hat, a ring, a scarf, a sweater, a shoe.

Take it off and you will feel liberated and more relaxed.

There is a strong link between emotional states and insights. *Happiness* increases our likelihood of experiencing them, whereas *anxiety* decreases it. When we are anxious, the activity in our brain increases, inhibiting our capacity to receive those subtle signals that occur right before an insight, when the brain becomes calm.

Other studies show that *people who have insights tend to be more aware of their inner experiences.* They are able to observe and change the way they think. They have more control over their thoughts, and are therefore more able to calm their minds. *According to scientific research, any technique or practice that helps us to know ourselves better, to develop our emotional intelligence, literally makes us more creative.* It isn't about focusing or concentrating more on the problem, nor do you need to be a genius to achieve this.

In short: anyone can find themselves blocked by an apparently insoluble problem, which in neuroscience is called an impasse. The key to getting out of an impasse is to give the brain a rest, reduce its activity, thereby preventing wrong solutions from appearing. For an insight to arise, we need to be able to detect extremely subtle signals, to allow the brain to make internal connections. And for that to happen, the brain has to be calm, with as little electrical activity as possible. For this reason, insights generally occur when we are more relaxed or contented. So, whenever you can, try to de-stress, reduce your anxiety levels by extending a deadline, taking a break, or doing something you enjoy. Let your mind slow down a bit to see whether any of those subtle connections appear. And if an insight does occur, focus on it as quickly as you can before that energy peak fades.

Random word exercise

Choose a word at random (or search online for a random word generator).

Draw what the word suggests to you. That way you will start using the right side of your brain.

Next to your drawing, write down all the attributes of your chosen word.

Then write down all the associations the word has for you.

Connect those attributes and associations with your creative challenge.

For example:

My challenge: to design a new toothbrush.

My random word: dog.

Attributes: hairy, black nose, four legs, wags its tail, buries bones.

Associations: affectionate, loyal, courageous, saves lives.

Combine attributes and associations with my creative challenge: How about a toothbrush that also gives you a face massage (wags its tail, affectionate)?

Relaxation

You have probably been reading for a while, taking in a lot of information. I suggest you stop for a moment and relax. Your brain has been extremely active, and now it deserves a short break. Take a few deep breaths and sit or lie down for five minutes. Let your thoughts flow freely. Close your eyes if you feel comfortable doing so.

What happened to your mind while you were doing this? You doubtless took a deep breath, but what did your mind do in the meantime? Did any thoughts arise? Of course they did. Were any of them interesting, practical or positive? Don't worry if they weren't. At moments like this, insights occur more frequently, when we are least expecting it.

Some researchers call this unfocused attention. As we have already seen, when there is less activity in our neural pathways, different neurons can become activated. In other words, if we relax a little, if we spread our net wide, we will catch a lot more fish.

Relaxation doesn't necessarily mean sitting still with your eyes closed. A lot of people relax when they are driving, enjoying themselves, talking about something unrelated to that elusive idea, walking, jogging or doing the washing up. People often feel relaxed in nature, but also when they paint, lie on the beach, or read. Some simply sit and meditate. We have already seen that the more mental clarity we have, the more ideas we generate. Studies suggest that relaxation can help boost creativity in two ways: by directly enhancing the creative process, and by lowering levels of stress, which inhibits creativity.

The most common brainwaves are beta waves, associated with our conscious, waking state. When we relax, the activity in the most highly specialised areas of our brain begins to slow down, and so-called alpha waves appear. Our mind wanders, and we start to daydream or fantasise. This often happens just before we fall asleep; our mind starts to drift and we imagine strange or nonsensical things.

When the neural activity of these highly specialised areas of the brain slows down, the brain as a whole starts to become more active. If I ask the trumpets in an orchestra to play more softly, I will hear the other instruments better. In the alpha state, neurons begin to charge up and fire off in all areas of the brain. When that happens, this new cerebral activity is dominated by gamma brainwaves, which, as we saw earlier, are directly related to the appearance of insights.

When our orchestra tunes up before a performance, all the instruments play different things simultaneously, producing a kind of musical chaos. Gamma brainwaves are a bit like that. They reveal, in a chaotic way, a heightened energy in the brain. And yet gamma brainwaves can also play harmoniously, like a high-energy symphonic orchestra. When that happens, thought processing occurs at an elevated level. Remote neural pathways cooperate and communicate, and the brain starts to assimilate complex information in order to identify and solve problems. When Buddhist monks meditate, they exhibit increased levels of synchronisation in the gamma brainwaves inside the association cortex. The regions of the association cortex aren't specialised, meaning they incorporate other areas of the brain. In states of deep relaxation, the specialised areas of the brain become quiet, and there is an increased activity in the non-specialised associative cortex. So, relaxation directly affects the creative process because when remote areas of the brain start to connect, it enables more insights to appear: distant drawers open and close, allowing memories to connect freely and in new ways, generating fresh ideas.

In the main, stress occurs when our survival mechanisms are on high alert. In that state we tend to make snap judgements or have knee-jerk reactions. We know that in order to be flexible enough to try out new ideas, we need to calm down and respond less quickly. Later on, we will see how emotions like stress depend hugely on a tiny area of the brain called the amygdala. Only five percent of all sensory stimuli passes through the amygdala, meaning that our brain frequently generates emotional responses based on little or limited information. Such responses directly influence what we think, and if we respond too quickly to our emotions and their associated thoughts, we risk perpetuating or exaggerating our emotional responses. We stop negotiating. We cling to our narrow perspective. We go into fight or flight mode. So it is helpful to allow our initial emotional response to calm down rather than to perpetuate itself.

We will look in more detail at how stress stimulates the production of cortisol, a hormone which destroys the cells in the hippocampus – the region of the brain essential for our capacity to store memories, but also for the acquisition of knowledge, the urge to explore.

In short, quiet walking, meditation, prayer or any other type of relaxing activity not only helps reduce stress and emotional reactivity, it also increases synchronisation and activity in the areas of the brain that are not specialised. This in turn gives the mind more space, enabling it to generate creative ideas or insights that arise from our unconscious.

Stars are invisible during the day because the light from the sun eclipses them. Similarly, many ideas remain undiscovered because, like tiny lights, they are eclipsed by the brain's activity.

This activity is known as beta wave activity. It is extremely noisy, like us when we munch on crisps. The deeper, slower alpha waves, which the brain produces at the precise moment when an insight occurs, are less noisy.

Alpha waves calm the mind, allowing us to 'see' solutions that are already there.

Four suggestions for enhancing your alpha waves:

▲ Sit in a quiet environment; in a room on your own or somewhere outside.

▲ Relaxation techniques. There are hundreds to choose from. If relaxation is new to you, choose a specific technique and try to practise it as often as possible.

▲ Adopt a passive attitude. Empty your mind. When thoughts arise, let them pass. Don't get caught up in them, or keep going over them in your head.

▲ Find a comfortable posture. Any posture that allows you to sit upright for fifteen minutes without falling asleep.

Just do it!

'Those who say it cannot be done shouldn't interrupt those doing it.'

Chinese proverb

When your boss asks you to think outside the box, does your heart sink, or do you feel an almost uncontrollable excitement because of the challenge it involves? When required to find a creative alternative to a specific problem, does your brain freeze up because you are afraid to try something new? Not everyone embraces change.

The risk involved in discovering fresh approaches can make us uneasy, and confronted with the challenges of everyday life we prefer to stick to tried-and-tested tools and solutions. Finding new ways to tackle problems isn't a hobby we take up voluntarily. Discarding old habits in order to see what is going on around us in a new light can be a challenge in itself. But it is by no means an insurmountable one. We only need look around us to see countless examples of people with a seemingly unlimited capacity to come up with fresh, creative challenges, whether in their professional or in their personal lives.

So, what is it that makes those people 'creative'? Put simply, they are creative because they want to be! Let's look at the person who sticks to the old ways compared to the one who blazes new trails. The person who embraces opportunity is already being creative, while the one who opts for the tried-and-tested path finds it much more difficult to get started; the fundamental difference between them is the desire to imagine things in a different way. If that key ingredient – 'desire' (the urge to look at the world through fresh ideas) – is missing, then it is almost impossible for us to think creatively.

Reason: friend or foe?

How do we process new information? In order to make sense of a seemingly nonsensical situation, most of us call upon our trusted ally: reason. Reason, we believe, enables us to reduce the risk of error while at the same time improving the quality of our decision-making. In fact, we feel confident, certain that we can distinguish between more or less viable ideas. Because we have thought about the problem 'rationally', it follows that we have come up with the most 'rational' solution. And yet, my idea of reason might differ from yours. Does that make me more rational than you? I doubt it. The fact is, I applied my notion of reason to a particular situation, but it turns out that your notion of reason is different! Not 'irrational', merely different. When faced with the challenges of everyday life, we often assess them using predetermined notions: how did I deal with this problem last time? We are too busy to make an in-depth logical analysis of every situation.

When confronted with the need to process new information, most of us automatically resort to predetermined ideas. This is a vital mechanism that allows us to respond adequately to the world around us using learned behaviour. But, fear of the unexpected, the unknown, can also blind us to new opportunities. Leaving our comfort zone is a daunting prospect because it implies risk. Sailing into uncharted territory can make us feel totally disoriented, and this lack of control over where we are going can block us, basically preventing the flow of our creative juices. Our need for control, based on the ease of using something that has worked for us before, inhibits the discovery of new possibilities.

Controlling the uncontrollable

Although control is necessary in some situations, outside influences constantly prevent us from controlling every aspect of our lives. The will of another may override our own, leaving us angry and frustrated. That anxiety can cloud our vision and cause us to feel needlessly stressed. Similarly, trying always to keep up with the latest trends can make us feel incomplete if we don't possess the most up-to-date digital devices, mobile phones, etc. As with our need to control, this constant search for material satisfaction can lead to frustration. The more we insist on control, the more external satisfaction we will need, and the more exposed we will be to unnecessary frustration.

By clinging to our habits, we rely on old assumptions, which in turn can limit our possibilities. Too much control is incompatible with a world in constant flux. And yet, as creatures of habit, we prefer to avoid change, allowing our decisions to be guided for the most part by learned behaviour and habits. However, once we accept that the world is constantly changing, and we adapt to that, we will be able to free ourselves to discover a new way of living or a new way of looking at old behaviour.

Finding freedom

As we have already seen, the process of 're-wiring' our brains to think outside the box, learning how to look at problems from a different perspective, and venturing into unknown territory, requires both energy and desire. This desire to explore new alternatives, to break with our old assumptions, provides us with the tools to go beyond the limitations of our habitual behaviour. How can we expect to progress if we never give new ideas a chance? If we succeed in overcoming the obstacle of our resistance, and allow ourselves the possibility of creative alternatives, we can unlock an infinite source of fresh opportunities. What once seemed unthinkable and filled us with dread will become a call to action, to try something new.

There is no denying that the creative path is fraught with difficulties, but if we choose to follow it we will experience an enormous sense of freedom in our personal as well as in our professional lives. The comfort we derive from ideas that have outgrown their usefulness can cause us to stagnate, preventing us from being able to imagine new alternatives. Creativity requires stimulation and incentive. We should treat this change of mind-set as a permanent learning curve, where we are constantly open to fresh and creative solutions.

Creative thinking allows us to experience new ideas, and that implies constantly adapting to change, in a place where the ground is permanently shifting beneath our feet! This sudden freedom brings with it the capacity to see the extraordinary in the ordinary. Too often, learned habits and behaviour determine the way we confront the challenges in our lives, but we know that change is possible if we give new ideas a chance.

All we have to do is light the spark of our desire for change!

'Your assumptions are your windows onto the world. Scrub them off every once in a while, or the light won't come in.'

Alan Alda

Reversing assumptions

We have assumptions about every subject, discipline or challenge: what is said, what is known, or what people believe should be true. Write down all the assumptions related to your creative challenge and then reverse them. What comes out of that?

The expert's blind spot

'Men can live without air for a few minutes, without water for about two weeks, without food for about two months – and without a new thought for years on end.'

Kent Ruth

Studies of highly creative thinkers show that they all have one thing in common: a degree of ability to tolerate ambiguity, dissonance, inconsistency and things that are out of place. These thinkers look at problems from different perspectives; they try to examine different variables, often looking for the unexpected. The more educated we are, the more ice cubes we have in our tray and the more specialised they become, and this can lead to our imagination becoming limited if we don't use it. Often, people who are more knowledgeable see less and people who are less knowledgeable see more. Leonardo da Vinci never went to university and his adult mind was more like a glass of water than a tray of ice cubes. His mind integrated information instead of segregating it.

Personal impasse

In 2004, I found myself at the Harvard School of Medicine studying a devastating genetic disease called Duchenne muscular dystrophy. I had gone to Boston in 2002 after finishing my PhD in France, and now here I was, two years later, faced with a dilemma: I had gathered a vast amount of information, but I couldn't advance with my research because I was having difficulty analysing my results. I had reached a huge, anxiety-inducing impasse. Despite everything I knew about muscles, molecular biology and the biochemistry of DMD, I couldn't understand the results I had obtained from my experiments. It was then, in a state of paralysis, that I resolved to do what we normally do when we have problems at work: consult someone more knowledgeable – in this case, my boss, Dr Louis Kunkel. Lou, as we called him, welcomed me into his office, where I spent the best part of three hours sifting through a huge pile of data and information in order to show him my results. It was Lou who, in 1988, had discovered the reason why children develop DMD; he was an expert in the field and his research had made him a likely candidate for the Nobel Prize. Lou was (and is) the person most liable to be able to help me. He spent those hours poring over my results with great application and determination, and finally he said:

'Look, Estani, the fact is I have no more idea than you what to do with everything you've shown me. There are lots of things I don't understand, and I can't tell you how to proceed, something eludes me, but I can't put my finger on it.'

Disillusioned by his words, imagine my astonishment when a moment later he added:

'Why not ask the janitors what they think about all this?'

The people employed to clean offices, schools and university buildings after everyone else has gone home? They arrive like an army equipped with buckets, mops, polishing machines and hoovers, leaving everything spotless overnight so that we – in our case the researchers and their teams – can come in the next day and do our jobs more easily.

'But, Lou,' I said, 'I don't understand. How am I going to explain something as complex as what we're doing here in the lab to people who know nothing about the subject?'

To which he replied, with a half-smile:

'Aren't they Spanish-speakers like you? Isn't Spanish your mother tongue?'

'Yes, of course, you're right. They are mostly immigrants from Guatemala, Honduras and El Salvador and Spanish-speakers like me,' I said.

'Good, then explain to them in your own language, in the simplest possible way, which I am sure you will do very well, about the problem areas in your results that are preventing you from making headway. You came to me for guidance, do what I suggest and then we'll talk,' Lou said to me.

I went away, somewhat anxious and baffled by his advice. I had been working in molecular biology for two years, and had been studying the subject in increasing depth. Now, for the first time, I had to face a completely new audience, with a totally different perspective, and I wasn't sure how to respond. I was used to giving classes to fellow biologists and doctors, and occasionally to business people in France and the United States, or during my flying visits to Argentina.

I confess that I had certain prejudices confronted with the task my boss had set me. But I also found it interesting, and hugely challenging. My Spanish-speaking colleagues encouraged me, and wanted to take part by sharing their own research too.

I started to stay on late at work so I could chat with the janitors, and I organised a meeting in the amphitheatre at the Boston Children's Hospital, a wonderful venue where Nobel

Prize winners and a host of other famous and successful speakers have been invited. Despite having been voted best lecturer in the Department of Biological Sciences at Harvard four months earlier, I was a bundle of nerves that evening. In addition, I had to speak in Spanish about a subject which for years I had only spoken about in English. This was a huge challenge.

At three a.m. on D-day, the janitors took a break and we gathered in the auditorium. About twenty-five people turned up, and it was moving to see them deposit their mops and buckets at the back of the amphitheatre, and sit down, possibly for the first time, in a place they were familiar with because they cleaned it every night. The show began. I tried to explain as clearly as possible, avoiding any technical jargon, what my problem was, and why I had asked them to come there. I did a PowerPoint presentation using illustrations, photographs and diagrams, summarising for them my two years of research. To begin with, they maintained a respectful silence, and then a few of them started to break the ice, posing simple but interesting questions aimed at finding out more about what I did. I couldn't help noticing a few admiring gazes, too, and I had the feeling I was more Latin American than Argentinian, at once close to and removed from them. Until a woman whom I remember was pregnant and from El Salvador stood up and asked me a question that caused something to go click in my head: it gave me an insight. Without going into detail (which isn't the aim of this book), I had shown them a few diagrams and explained that according to the biochemical technique I was using, the presence of some black spots meant that the thing I was interested in finding in the patients' samples wasn't there. The woman from El Salvador asked me an interesting question:

'I don't understand. You say that when you see something – those black spots – it means nothing is there. If you are showing me a spot then that spot must mean something is there.'

Her words made me travel back two years, to when I first set up my experiments, and caused me to ask myself the following question: What if I had made a mistake with the chemical reagents and the equipment involved in developing this technique? It quickly occurred to me that such a mistake might explain the inconsistency of my results, and consequently my dilemma about how to proceed with my research (an 'error carried forward' as it's called in mathematics). My meeting with the janitors went on a bit longer, but I kept thinking about the woman's question, and when I got back to the lab I hurriedly looked over my notes from two years before, the reagents I had used and my preparations. That is why it is essential in science to write down and log everything you do. That very night I repeated my experiment of two years ago, naturally taking great care this time over how I mixed the reagents and chemicals, and my use of the equipment. Two or three weeks later, it started to become clear. I had indeed made a mistake, and the perspective of someone who couldn't have been more removed from my field, enabled me to have that revelation and get to the bottom of it. The result was the publication of two internationally acclaimed science papers.

When we know a subject well, when we have a lot of experience, when we understand the culture of a discipline (in my case molecular biology), a country, a company, a family, we have many certainties. And this is a good thing. However, knowing about something often restricts our mind, because it prevents us from looking further, from realising that other possibilities exist or that a question can have several answers. As I said before, experience generally helps us to solve problems we come across on a daily basis, the same way we did in the past, and the perspective of someone who isn't an expert, or who comes from another discipline, sometimes allows us to find a different possible solution to the problem confronting us.

Total opposites

Occasionally the most interesting or fertile ideas arise from components of subjects totally different or directly opposed to the themes we are dealing with in our creative challenge.

For example, if my job is events organiser, and my challenge is 'to make parties for young people more entertaining', I might make a list of attributes or characteristics related to a church.

As I start to list these attributes, my mind will come up with interesting and amusing associations, which I will be able to adapt to my creative challenge.

Test your creativity

(adapted from Josh Linkner's blog)

Answer the following questions as honestly as you can on a scale of 1 to 5. As you choose your answer, print each number in the results chart at the end of the list of questions.

1) I bring my creativity with me wherever I go (to meetings, talks, and in interactions with other people). It is an essential part of who I am.

Strongly agree	Agree	Neutral	Disagree	Strongly disagree
1	2	3	4	5

2) Before I start any project that requires creativity, I am always clear about what my creative aims are.

Strongly agree	Agree	Neutral	Disagree	Strongly disagree
1	2	3	4	5

3) I am comfortable about sharing my opinions and taking certain risks at work or in my studies.

Strongly agree	Agree	Neutral	Disagree	Strongly disagree
1	2	3	4	5

4) I rarely lack sources of creativity. I always have plenty of sources that inspire me.

Strongly agree	Agree	Neutral	Disagree	Strongly disagree
1	2	3	4	5

5) My ideas are very different to those of my colleagues or friends.

Strongly agree	Agree	Neutral	Disagree	Strongly disagree
1	2	3	4	5

6) In teamwork, the best idea should win, not that of the 'expert' on the subject.

Strongly agree	Agree	Neutral	Disagree	Strongly disagree
1	2	3	4	5

7) I feel an abundance of creativity inside me.

Strongly agree	Agree	Neutral	Disagree	Strongly disagree
1	2	3	4	5

8) I regularly question and challenge the way things are.

Strongly agree	Agree	Neutral	Disagree	Strongly disagree
1	2	3	4	5

9) I routinely do mental warm-up activities before confronting my creative challenges.

Strongly agree	Agree	Neutral	Disagree	Strongly disagree
1	2	3	4	5

10) I work quickly and easily when facing a creative challenge.

Strongly agree	Agree	Neutral	Disagree	Strongly disagree
1	2	3	4	5

11) I frequently carry out brainstorming sessions in a fun, focused, productive way.

Strongly agree	Agree	Neutral	Disagree	Strongly disagree
1	2	3	4	5

12) I have a system for selecting the best ideas from the not-so-good ones.

Strongly agree	Agree	Neutral	Disagree	Strongly disagree
1	2	3	4	5

13) Where I work, we are expected to be creative, whatever the task in hand.

Strongly agree	Agree	Neutral	Disagree	Strongly disagree
1	2	3	4	5

14) I often find myself wondering why some things haven't yet been invented.

Strongly agree	Agree	Neutral	Disagree	Strongly disagree
1	2	3	4	5

15) When working on new ideas, I leave my everyday environment and find a new one that enables me to be creative.

Strongly agree	Agree	Neutral	Disagree	Strongly disagree
1	2	3	4	5

16) I feel confident enough to cope with any kind of creative challenge, big or small.

Strongly agree	Agree	Neutral	Disagree	Strongly disagree
1	2	3	4	5

17) When working alone or in a group in order to develop new ideas, I employ different techniques that draw on my creative potential.

Strongly agree	Agree	Neutral	Disagree	Strongly disagree
1	2	3	4	5

18) I know how to gauge the level of creativity in my ideas.

Strongly agree	Agree	Neutral	Disagree	Strongly disagree
1	2	3	4	5

19) Where I work or study, creativity is encouraged, valued and rewarded.

Strongly agree	Agree	Neutral	Disagree	Strongly disagree
1	2	3	4	5

20) I seldom accept the way things are, and I frequently question authority.

Strongly agree	Agree	Neutral	Disagree	Strongly disagree
1	2	3	4	5

21) When I create new things, I rarely edit or change them as I go along.

Strongly agree	Agree	Neutral	Disagree	Strongly disagree
1	2	3	4	5

22) I know plenty of techniques that stimulate creativity.

Strongly agree	Agree	Neutral	Disagree	Strongly disagree
1	2	3	4	5

23) I am very imaginative and come up with lots of 'crazy' ideas.

Strongly agree	Agree	Neutral	Disagree	Strongly disagree
1	2	3	4	5

24) Once I have a good idea, I usually test it out before sharing it with others.

Strongly agree	Agree	Neutral	Disagree	Strongly disagree
1	2	3	4	5

25) Creativity, originality and imagination are on my list of personal and professional priorities.

Strongly agree	Agree	Neutral	Disagree	Strongly disagree
1	2	3	4	5

26) I am highly aware of my environment and surroundings.

Strongly agree	Agree	Neutral	Disagree	Strongly disagree
1	2	3	4	5

27) I feel comfortable about taking risks and contributing innovative ideas, with no fear of embarrassment.

Strongly agree	Agree	Neutral	Disagree	Strongly disagree
1	2	3	4	5

28) I frequently use metaphors or analogies.

Strongly agree	Agree	Neutral	Disagree	Strongly disagree
1	2	3	4	5

29) I have a good system for generating new ideas for any type of challenge.

Strongly agree	Agree	Neutral	Disagree	Strongly disagree
1	2	3	4	5

30) When I create good ideas, I know how to put them into practice.

Strongly agree	Agree	Neutral	Disagree	Strongly disagree
1	2	3	4	5

Scoring

Step 1: Write the reply to each question on the right of the corresponding number on the chart:

	A		B		C		D		E		F
1		2		3		4		5		6	
7		8		9		10		11		12	
13		14		15		16		17		18	
19		20		21		22		23		24	
25		26		27		28		29		30	
Total		Total		Total		Total		Total		Total	
			Overall total								

Step 2: Add up the total of each column. This will give you a score for columns A, B, C, D, E, F.

Step 3: Add up the points from the five columns to obtain your total score.

The results

Based on the total number of points scored, let's look at the results obtained:

130–150: You are in a better position than most. This score places you in the top ten percent of creative individuals (and organisations). You are in touch with your creativity and work in an organisation that supports it. This score also means you are well placed to continue to develop your creative capacity and are on your way towards achieving your maximum potential.

110–129: Not bad at all, although there is definite room for improvement. This score suggests that you are doing many things right, but that there are also substantial barriers to your creativity. It could be that you work in an organisation that is impeding and inhibiting you. This score range should alert you to your potential, which you may not be taking full advantage of.

85–109: Unfortunately, you are in the same situation as about sixty percent of the population. You probably have significant creative abilities, but they are being severely limited most of the time. Perhaps the management in your organisation is holding you back, or you have a lot of beliefs that limit your desire to express your creative abilities. You may tell yourself that you aren't creative or that people will laugh at you if you share your ideas. Your creativity muscles are in need of a vigorous work out. The good news is that once you start exercising your creativity, you will quickly notice significant improvements.

84 or less: Creatively, you are in the danger zone. This score should serve as a wake-up call, a sign that unless you make some radical changes, you are storing up trouble for yourself in the future. You are in creative limbo and need to reconnect instantly with your imagination. Perhaps your work or routine are holding you back. This information might sound alarming, but don't be disheartened.

Bear in mind that these scores are an indicator of where you are now in contrast to your potential. They are a reflection of that potential, and are intended to serve as a starting point on your path towards greater creativity.

Now let's look at the scores from each column, A to F, which reflect your current strengths and weaknesses in specific areas. Each column has a maximum of 25 points. This is how the scores are broken down:

22–25: Excellent
19–21: Above average
17–18: Average
16 or less: Below average

The score in each column represents a different element of your creative capacity.

Column A: corresponds to general aspects of your intentions with regard to creativity.

Column B: indicates your level of curiosity and attentiveness.

Column C: shows how well you prepare your environment and your mind to enable your ideas to flow better.

Column D: indicates how good you are at finding creative ideas and taking inspiration from different areas of your life. (Conceptual blending.)

Column E: shows how capable you are of generating a lot of good ideas when necessary.

Column F: indicates how able you are to select the best ideas and put your creativity into practice.

Remember: these scores are only designed to offer you a glimpse of your current situation and which areas you need to focus on more in order to grow.

THE SENSES

I perceive that you sense me

One of the pillars of creativity is the stimulation of the senses. We cannot hope to switch on and develop our creativity unless we are open and ready to perceive things as if for the first time. Avoiding stereotypes with a fresh perception is what enables us to deploy our creativity fully.

Perception is the process whereby our brain experiences the outside world through our senses. We use sight, hearing, touch, smell and taste to understand our environment, to gather information, or stimuli, from our surroundings. The brain uses those stimuli to formulate ideas and opinions, assess situations, generate responses and then store what is learned in our memory.

Although for many years this was thought to be a passive process, a growing body of scientific evidence suggests that perception doesn't only register or record, it also constructs reality. This construction depends on the one observing reality; a person's perception depends on his or her assumptions. In other words, we experience different aspects of things; everyone's perception is slightly different.

Let's take the Niagara Falls. Some people would say: 'Isn't this mighty waterfall one of God's most miraculous creations?' Others will have a different perception: 'It is Nature which constructed this miracle'. A water sports enthusiast might think: 'What a great challenge it would be to go over the top in a raft'. A person in the hotel business would remark: 'What an amazing place to have a hotel or a restaurant'. A geography buff would think of them as the perfect place to pursue their hobby. A painter would say: 'What a beautiful place to find inspiration and paint'. A geologist might want to venture into the caves behind the falls.

A famous quote by Picasso arose out of his encounter with a stranger at an exhibition of the artist's work in a Paris museum. The man approached him and said: 'Why don't you paint people the way they appear?' Picasso replied: 'And how do they appear?' Upon which the man took out of his wallet a photograph of his wife and showed it to the artist. Picasso looked at it and said: 'She's incredibly short, isn't she? And thin.' He was referring, of course, to the photograph, not to the man's wife. We have to accept that the reality we see is influenced by our own perceptions.

Every scrap of information that enters our brain through the senses has a powerful effect on our thoughts, our emotions, our personality, and consequently on our creativity. There are specialised neurons that govern our responses to different stimuli or changes in our environment. Perception is our interpretation of what a stimulus means to us. For example, if I hear music, I might notice that it's very loud or that it's one of my favourite songs. Astonishingly, the brain processes the majority of the outside stimuli we receive unconsciously. Our five senses capture approximately eleven million bits of information per second, most of it visual, and yet our conscious brain is only able to process around forty bits per second.

As the brain gathers information from the outside world, it becomes habituated to patterns of perception, much like the dominant thought patterns we have already looked at. When we encounter a breed of dog we have never seen before, our brain processes the animal's shape and size, the smell, colour and texture of its fur, and many other details. At that moment, our brain concludes that it is seeing a new breed of dog. When we come across that breed again, our brain will make the connection with what it is seeing almost instantaneously. In other words, our brain will begin categorising all the fresh mental images in accordance with what it has seen and experienced previously. This is what Walter Lippmann called 'stereotyping', and it is crucial for our day-to-day understanding and survival; imagine if at each moment we had to analyse the accumulation of information and sensory minutiae in our environment.

Each of us filters what happens around us in a particular way and can transform a city street into a symphony of light and sound or into a hideous eyesore. The brain frequently simplifies our perceptions so that we can spend the day more efficiently. Stereotyping anticipates our actions and reactions and prepares us to minimise or maximise pleasure. Stereotyping a dog's growl or bark will tell our brain whether the animal is a threat or not. As Lippmann said: 'We do not see first, and then define; we define first and then see'.

Even our imagination isn't safe

If I ask you to imagine a sunset on Pluto and then to draw it, your drawing will almost certainly resemble a sunset on earth, with a few possible variations in colour or features of the planet. You may use your imagination freely to create whatever you want, and yet you will doubtless think of something similar to what you already know as a sunset. This phenomenon is known as *structured imagination*, which means that even when using our imagination to develop new ideas, these ideas will be heavily structured in predictable ways according to pre-existing concepts, categories and stereotypes in our mind. This befalls artists as much as writers, designers, business people or anyone who is simply daydreaming.

In order to explore beyond the limits of the concepts we have already incorporated into separate categories, we need to destructure our imagination. Mix the ice cubes and let them melt together. In order to achieve that, we must look at ideas and concepts that are unrelated to our challenge – what we referred to earlier as conceptual blending. At first you may find this detrimental or removed from your actual challenge, but with time and practice you will see that it is an excellent and creative way of resolving problems. Ideally, we should allow ourselves to think the unthinkable. However, the brain basically dislikes ambiguity. Its primary function is to reduce the complexity of our experience.

When the mind is forced to focus on a specific object or theme, it gets bored after a while and starts looking for other ways of perceiving it; for example, breaking it down into its constituent parts which it then examines to see if anything interesting arises. When we are in a class, after a while we stop concentrating. Our attention begins to focus on details, for example the clothes the teacher is wearing, how he or she moves, which hand he or she uses to write on the board. No doubt we will discover something in this breakdown that pleases us: a smile, a tone of voice. It seems that the same thing happens during the thought process. When we think up an idea, no matter how absurd or silly, our mind begins to break it down into different parts, looking for what is interesting in order to construct fresh ideas relating to our challenge. As we already saw, this occurs below the threshold of consciousness, but after a while it begins to permeate our consciousness in the form of fresh insights. This destructuring of the imagination enables us to dare to imagine that we can achieve the impossible.

Think of something you consider impossible and try to come up with ideas that would bring it into the realm of what is possible. For example, imagine that your mobile phone is a living, breathing creature. List the attributes of living creatures (they are born, they reproduce, they grow, they feel, etc.)

You might use these attributes to come up with a new design for a mobile phone (one that senses when you are unwell, responds to the weather, and so on).

Continued

Forcing your imagination to try to make the impossible possible through concrete thoughts and actions is the opposite of the way dreams work. Dreams represent abstract ideas through concrete images and actions, while the creative process uses concrete ideas (for example a living mobile phone) in order to obtain insights and discover novel thoughts and ideas (such as a mobile phone that expresses feelings).

READY, AIM… IMAGINE

When our imagination compares a problem (your creative challenge) with something unusual, it establishes a need for that comparison to mean something. This generates fresh connections and associations, which enable us to produce a futuristic, novel, creative idea.

Other questions to stimulate your imagination:

What would happen if you could eat walnuts at breakfast? What would happen if our genitals were on our foreheads? What would happen if the taller you grew, the more beautiful and intelligent you became? What would happen if the winners of conflicts between different countries were those able to make its people laugh the most? What would happen if we slept for twenty-three hours and were only awake for one? What would happen if trees started to produce vast quantities of petrol? What would happen if you changed sex? What would happen if humans lived forever? How would that affect us as individuals, our businesses, our religions etc.? What would happen if our eyes were in our neck? What would happen if everyone with a job adopted a homeless person and looked after him or her for the rest of their lives? What animal resembles my problem? Why? In what way does my problem resemble a torch with no batteries? If my problem were a lawn, which part would be the weeds? How could a fizzy drink that has gone flat and has been standing in the sun for two hours be the solution to my problem?

You can relate your answers to your creative challenge or simply use them as a mental warming-up exercise.

When neurons are frequently exposed to particular stimuli, we learn from these experiences. They become established in specific regions of the brain, from which we are able to process them automatically with a minimum of cognitive effort. A child can distinguish its mother's voice from among many, a musician can hear and differentiate between the different instruments in an orchestra, and a dog instantly knows that the sound of the lead means it is going for a walk. In contrast, new experiences increase neural connections, construct other synaptic patterns and enhance our perception of the world. New information and new experiences keep our brain in good shape as if we were exercising a muscle. If you do something for the first time in your life, you are developing your brain, increasing its connections.

In short: perception is the function of the brain that enables us, through the senses, to receive, develop and interpret information coming from our surroundings.

A few simple ways of enhancing our perception

Estimate things. For example, time: how long will it take me to get from one place to another? How long will I have to wait in the queue at the bank or the cinema? Estimate size: what is the height,

Continued

length and width of an object? What object will fit into what space? Estimate volumes: how much of something will fit into a container? Estimate distances: how far is it until I reach my destination? How far is it to the corner or the traffic light? Estimate weight: how much does a piece of fruit weigh, or a bag of lemons? How much does a bag or box weigh? Try to guess how a person will act in a specific situation and then compare what you thought would happen with what actually happened.

Our imagination and creativity also improve when our brain responds to new perceptions, especially if we attempt to experience the world in novel ways. Walk to new places, where your senses will smell, hear and see things you have never experienced before. Explore all the artefacts in a museum. Listen to complex music and let your mind interpret the patterns. Music stimulates many areas of the brain and gives us opportunities to create fresh neural connections. Research by the neurologist Richard Restak suggests that listening to Mozart for a few minutes every day can boost our knowledge on several levels, from simple perceptions to more profound thoughts.

Look out!

Henri Matisse said: 'The artist begins with a vision – a creative operation requiring an effort'. And he was ahead of his time. We now know that our visual experience isn't a passive activity, but rather one that develops through analysing different streams of information which include colour, movement, external shapes, etc.

Each of these is processed in a separate but simultaneous way before being gathered together and synthesised in different regions of the brain. What we perceive visually is the end product of a long and complex assembly line. This process of construction starts when the information we see (the raw material) is sent to the region in the back of our brain. From there it splits into two paths that go to different areas, where colour, shape and size will be processed. Finally, all these elements will come together to form the 'end' image that makes sense to us.

At least a quarter of the brain is involved in the visual process, much more than with any of our other senses. What's more, our eyes contain seventy percent of all the body's sense receptors. In other words, essentially we understand the world around us by looking at it. A well-known experiment carried out at the University of Bordeaux consisted of presenting a group of expert wine tasters with some white wine to which had been added an odourless, tasteless, red colourant. Their smell and taste was duped by the colour of the wine, which they described in language appropriate to a red wine. Another experiment using nuclear magnetic resonance reveals the power vision exerts over the other senses: when subjects were shown video footage of people conversing with the sound turned down, their auditory cortex lit up, whereas images of people making faces elicited no such response.

As we mentioned previously, vision occurs not in our eyes, but in our brains. Our eyes capture and focus light, but it is our brain that gives meaning to colours, shapes and facial expressions. This explains how we are able to recall scenes accurately months or years after they occur, and why we can 'see' some of the things we imagine, or why our dreams are so vivid. We have all heard the old saying 'a picture is worth a thousand words', and the reason for it is that images and words follow different rules in the brain.

Experiments show that people can remember in excess of two thousand five hundred images with more than ninety percent accuracy several days after seeing them, even when they are only shown an image for ten seconds. After a year the recall of those images is seventy three percent. In the memory stakes, images beat written and oral presentations hands down. After three days, we can remember barely ten percent of an oral presentation. If we add an image, that average increases to sixty-five percent. It has been amply demonstrated that multisensory learning approaches are much more efficient than unisensory ones. Written presentations fare much worse than oral ones, because the brain perceives words as lots of tiny images. We don't see words, we see minuscule drawings with hundreds of different shapes. This means that for the most evolved region of our brain, the prefrontal cortex, words don't exist, they are images. One possible reason for this is that our evolutionary history was governed not by letters in Times New Roman font, but by the leaves on trees, and hungry leopards. The moment we stood erect on two legs, vision became our dominant sense. Through it we could scan our surroundings more efficiently for predators, movements, food, water sources, opportunities to procreate, and so on. When discussing evolution, studying babies is the best way of understanding more about ourselves. If we fasten a ribbon with a tiny bell to the leg of a baby less than one year old, we will see that at first the baby appears to move the leg randomly. However, it will soon learn that moving the leg with the bell attached makes a tinkling sound, and it will cheerfully begin moving that leg more than the other. If we remove the bell, and place it to one side, the baby will continue to kick that leg with increasing force, despite the absence of any sound, and to look unsuccessfully at the discarded bell. The baby's visual response tells us that he/she is paying attention to the problem. We are now able to use technology to measure attention in young infants, and it has been observed that from an early age babies start to learn about the relationship between cause and effect. Their brains come equipped with a degree of visual processing software, so that they can already see certain things without being taught. This 'software' has a predilection for patterns with lots of contrast, because they allow us to see that objects moving together form part of a whole, like the black and white stripes of a zebra, for example. We are able to distinguish from an early age between human and non-human faces – and we prefer the former, obviously. We are able to understand size in relation to distance. When an object approaches, it becomes bigger but is still the same object.

In other words, our tendency towards a predominantly visual behaviour begins when we are very young. When seventy year olds are asked about their most vivid memories, the majority will remember events from when they were between fifteen and thirty, which is why it is thought that the peak of our visual memory occurs around that age. One possible explanation for this is that it is a very dynamic period of our lives. Finally, there are several examples of how our visual experience of what we consider beautiful influences the decisions we make: studies show that better-looking criminals receive shorter sentences, cuter babies receive better attention in clinics, and a good-looking person is more likely to be awarded a job than a less good-looking candidate with the same CV.

The neurologist Richard Restak suggests a few ways in which we can use vision to expand the sensory networks in our brain and to develop our creativity and memory. One of his best-known ideas is the bonsai technique.

The bonsai technique

Place a bonsai tree on the floor and look at it from above, trying to memorise the shapes and patterns of each of its branches. Close your eyes and try to 'see it' using your memory. Open your eyes and check how well you have done. Repeat the exercise with the bonsai tree at eye level, only now attempt to zoom in and count the number of branches. Count the exact number of leaves on each branch. Close your eyes and recreate the image in your mind. Focus your thought on images not words. As you improve your ability to 'see' the details of the bonsai with your eyes open or closed, you are strengthening the neural networks involved in perception.

It's time for you to put this book aside, stretch out on the floor, close your eyes and let your imagination take flight. Closing your eyes will shut down a large area of your brain which is dedicated to visual stimulation, enabling you to activate and connect other regions. Focus on your breath, on an image of somewhere pleasant (I like to imagine a snow-covered mountain in the warm sunshine) or on a sound. Lots of different thoughts will invade your consciousness. Don't fight them. Let them come and go. Imagine the mind as a path where thoughts arise and disappear. It is possible that with practice you will succeed in emptying that path completely (some people achieve this after a few attempts, some after a dozen, some never). When that happens, I guarantee you (based on personal experience, and there are scientific studies to back me up) that gradually you will start to have more creative ideas. Experts recommend you practise this exercise twice a day for twenty minutes. If the subject interests you, I suggest you find out more about transcendental meditation or have a look at David Lynch's book *Catching the Big Fish*.

I love green

Some studies show that simply placing flowers and plants in an office increases the ideas generated by employees by up to fifteen percent. Replacing them with images or posters of nature doesn't produce the same effect. Researchers also discovered that the games played by children in spaces where there is vegetation are much more inventive than those played by children in spaces with no vegetation. There is a substantial improvement in the recovery time of patients in hospitals who are able to see trees from their windows. Prisoners whose cells overlook a field or forest complain of fewer ailments than other prisoners.

A group of people was asked to solve some anagrams. On the sheet of paper they were given, half of their names were printed in red on the top right-hand corner and the other half in green. Participants were asked to check that their names had been spelled correctly, thus assuring that they would see the colour red or green before tackling the anagrams. Those whose names were printed in green solved thirty percent more of the anagrams than those whose names were printed in red. The results suggest that green is a better colour for being creative. The researchers think that red is widely associated with the sensation of danger, mistakes, traffic lights, teachers grading with a red pen, and that green is associated with positivity, nature, etc. If you can't see much green from your office or your bedroom window, when you redecorate go for more green rather than red; the same applies to carpets, chairs, clothes, desks, and so on.

And blue too…

The University of British Columbia asked six hundred participants to solve a series of cognitive tests printed on red, blue or neutral (black and white) backgrounds. Those given tests with a red background did much better at responding to tasks that required more precision and attention to detail; because red is associated with danger they were probably more alert. Those given tests with a blue background scored lower on short-term memory, but much higher on tests requiring imagination. According to scientists, the colour blue instantly triggers associations with the sky and the sea. We think of distant horizons, hazy sunlight, tropical beaches and days spent relaxing. Perfect for increasing alpha brain waves.

Relax and listen

The brain also gathers vital information from the environment through noises and sounds. When we hear dripping water, two cars colliding, or hailstones falling, we know something is happening before we are able to see it. We possess a kind of sensor that enables us to judge the source of a sound, how far away it is and where it is coming from. The vibrations, or sound waves, which enter our ears are first transformed into electrical signals. After a complex process, they end up in the auditory cortex, where the frequency, intensity, quality and meaning of the sound are processed. The main characteristics that influence our perception of sound are frequency (number of vibrations per second) and amplitude (the size of the peaks and troughs of the sound waves). If we had to differentiate between noise and music, we would say that noise produces sound with irregular wave patterns and music produces sound with harmonic ones. In cases where a sound range comprises different degrees of intensity and tone, other groups of specialised cells vibrate in resonance, so that the auditory cortex processes two or more sounds. That is what happens when we differentiate between the instruments in an orchestra. The brain captures all the sounds at a party in which a large group of people is talking and shouting with music playing in the background. However, we are able to follow the thread of a conversation because the auditory cortex can detect which sounds are meaningful and what is mere noise. Other sounds that are essential to human beings are a mother's heartbeat and breathing, which has a calming effect on babies. Sounds frequently generate nostalgic memories associated with the past (such as the music of our youth). The important phases of our lives are often accompanied by music (marriage, graduation, death, etc.), and when we sing our pupils dilate and we secrete endorphins. Patients in coma respond to music, and terminal patients relax with it. On a more commercial level, the jingle accompanying a consumer product or service or the sounds we associate with it can intensify the pleasure we experience (a can of fizzy drink being opened, coffee being poured, the crunch of crisps, the tokens at a casino, for example).

> Subconscious insights are like a mobile phone ringing at a loud party: you can't hear them above the background noise created by your prefrontal cortex. Only by relaxing will you be able to hear what your subconscious is saying. Doubtless it brings good news for your creative challenge.

That smells good

Smell is the oldest of the five senses and the only one, which, unlike hearing, sight, touch and taste, travels straight to our amygdala and our olfactory cortex, bypassing the thalamus. The reason for this is because, in evolutionary terms, smell was responsible for informing us quickly whether a potential food source had a bad smell and might be harmful to us. We are still good at detecting toxic chemicals, rotten food, etc. With the exception of exquisite French cheeses.

Almost any animal without a developed sense of smell is most likely to die before it can produce offspring. Generally speaking, predators like the smell of their quarry (the aroma of roast meat) whereas they smell bad to their quarry (lions smell repulsive to humans). Smells can also be a sign of disease, and this is why dogs are sometimes used to detect melanomas, epilepsy, low blood sugar, heart attacks; diabetes smells like sugar and measles smells of feathers. Man's best friend has two hundred and twenty million olfactory cells, compared to our five million.

The direct connection between the olfactory cortex and the amygdala exists because the amygdala can influence our heart rate and blood pressure as much as our feeling of calm and wellbeing; some smells cause anxiety while others are pleasant and enticing, such as those associated with aromatherapy.

Furthermore, there is a direct connection between our olfactory system and our emotional memory. You should smell good if you want people to remember you! Although smell takes up only one percent of our brain, if we are exposed to a familiar or evocative smell, we relive the emotions we experienced the first time we smelled it. The advertising world uses childhood smells that evoke powerful memories in order to make people associate a brand or product with pleasurable aromas.

Studies carried out in the business world have produced some amusing facts. For example, the scent of lemon increases seafood orders in restaurants, the smell of grass or soil close to the dairy counter in supermarkets increases sales, because it evokes freshness and the smells of the countryside. The leather used in luxury cars or luggage is associated with reward and relaxation. In some clothing companies, the smell of the sea, roses and violets increases sales. In the real estate business, the aroma of freshly baked biscuits entices potential buyers to make a purchase. In women's lingerie, the smell of vanilla triples sales, and the scent of honey and roses produces the same effect in underwear for men.

Apparently, the peak age for retaining pleasant smells occurs between five and ten, which is when we experience many smells for the first time. Childhood memories represent a time when we were free from responsibility and the habitual anxieties of adulthood. When those memories are unleashed through smells, we tend to idealise them, even if our childhood wasn't particularly idyllic. Being able to unearth them as adults often feels like a luxury. Doesn't the smell of freshly baked bread or chocolate biscuits remind us of the good old days when our grandma was still alive? Marcel Proust described how the aroma of madeleine cakes dipped in tea transported him back to his aunt's house when he was a child. 'When nothing else endures from the past, after the people are dead, after the things are broken and scattered, the smell and taste of things remain poised a long time, like souls, bearing resiliently on tiny almost impalpable drops of their essence, the immense edifice of memory.'

In the Starbucks chain, for example, employees aren't allowed to wear perfume because it might interfere with the tempting aroma of coffee, which attracts potential customers. One company found that sales from vending machines that give off an aroma of chocolate are sixty percent bigger.

Various studies show that women's smell is more sensitive than men's, and they find it easier to put a name to what they are smelling. Smell also plays an important role in taste. Much of our enjoyment of a good meal is due to our sense of smell, the chemical information we receive about what we are chewing, or even cutting up with a knife and fork. That information is ten thousand times more sensitive than the actual taste of the food. A life with no sense of smell is comparable to seeing a film in black and white as opposed to in full HD colour. A curious fact: our noses contain pain receptors, and some smells, like ammonia or very hot peppers, actually hurt.

The neurologist Richard Restak suggests families or friends explore a variety of fragrances together so that they impact positively on their emotional memory. A similar exercise would be to ask your dinner guests to bring their favourite fragrance with them. Pass the fragrances around amongst your guests and get them to explain why they prefer one and what memories they associate with it.

In the Design Department at Stanford University, smells are used to awaken memories and generate ideas; students are also encouraged to visualise problems in different colours and to use ink stains to get inspiration.

I like you

Do you remember the last time you had a cold or flu? Doubtless your food lost some of its taste while you were ill. That is because approximately three-quarters of what the brain perceives as taste actually enters through the nose. Taste also protects us from potential toxins, causing reactions such as vomiting or retching when we dislike something.

The first thing we 'savour' is breast milk, which creates the desire for warm, sweet food. (Our introduction to the world of taste is wonderful: warmth, tenderness, caresses and love.) The receptors on our tongue are able to distinguish five different tastes: sweet, bitter, salty, sour and umami. Umami was the word used by a Japanese chemistry professor called Kikunae Ikeda in 1908 to describe the taste of seaweed. In fact its receptors are found not on the tongue but in the pharynx. Beef, lamb, soy sauce, tomatoes and Parmesan cheese also contain umami components. Certain savoury, fatty and sugary foods, including sweets, release endorphins into the brain which act as mood enhancers. A craving for carbohydrates indicates the need to increase levels of serotonin, the calming hormone. Experiments with twins indicate that cravings are genetic: identical twins that are separated at birth develop the same cravings, whereas the same isn't true of non-identical twins.

Keep in touch

At first glance, in comparison with sight or smell, touch appears less important. However, for a baby it can make the difference between life and death. Human contact plays a crucial role in development. According to James Prescott, an expert in development, the quickest way to induce depression and alienation in a child is never to touch, hold or carry it. Prescott suggests that extremely violent societies arise due to inadequate bonding or union between mothers and their children based on touch.

During the thirteenth century, the Holy Roman Emperor Frederick II, in his search to discover the basic origins of human language, ordered a group of newborns to be educated without the use of language. The wet nurses who looked after them were also forbidden to touch them. All the babies died before they were able to speak.

Touch develops earlier than the other senses in the mother's womb. The way babies turn their head when their cheek is touched, the 'search' reflex, helps them to find the nipple during breastfeeding. We could say that there is a direct relationship between touch and the early stages of intelligence. Every sense has an organ, but in the case of touch the organ is our skin. Our skin is indispensable to our survival and development; it separates us from others, gives us our shape, protects us from germs, cools or warms us, produces Vitamin D, sustains our body fluids, heals itself, and is the body's largest organ. Touch receptors for sensing pressure, temperature, pain, vibrations, etc., can be found all over our skin in differing concentrations. In other words, according to how many receptors they have and where they are placed on our skin, different parts of our body vary in sensitivity to touch or painful stimuli. Compare lips and elbows, for example, or fingers and tongues – which are much more sensitive than backs. We obtain lots of information from touching a surface with our finger, and when we kiss our neuron activity goes into overdrive. Each square centimetre of skin contains, on average, approximately two thousand pain receptors, fifteen pressure receptors, six cold receptors and one heat receptor. Clearly the need to sense pain properly is vital for our survival, and our response to it is instantaneous.

Many pain receptors both detect and avoid pain. In 1990, a study of brain mapping was carried out on people who were blind and could read Braille. Not only did they feel the raised letters by activating touch pathways in their brain, they also recruited neurons from their visual cortex to help decipher them.

It is strange that even the most ticklish people in the world can't tickle themselves. This is because the brain controls your movements and anticipates the result; you know where you are going to put your fingers and what you will feel. The part of the brain called the cerebellum is responsible for distinguishing your own fingers from those of another whose actions it cannot predict and which lead to the sensation of ticklishness.

In social situations such as parties or dinner parties, French people may touch one another as many as two hundred times in half an hour, and the Americans four hundred times. No experiments have been carried out on Argentinians, but I daresay we would beat the record, or at least we would come second after the Brazilians. Finally, without a developed sense of touch, we would have no relationships and no children. We would disappear as a species. With good reason, sex is the greatest touch-related pleasure. The aim of our species to search for maximum pleasure was one of nature's greatest inventions.

'In my mind's eye,' Hamlet said to Horatio, and the phrase has become a common saying. In 2011, scientists in California under the direction of Antonio Damasio (a leading light in brain research) discovered that when we look at an object, our brain not only remembers its appearance, but also what it feels like to the touch. We could call this 'our mind's touch'. The evidence is so overwhelming that when we examine data from the part of the brain that processes touch, we can guess what object is being seen. In the same study, participants, who were connected to a powerful nuclear MRI scanner, were asked to imagine the difference between stroking the warm fur of a cat and a cold metal bar. They said they could 'feel' the difference, and in accordance with their declarations the area of their brain that lit up corresponded to the one that lights up when we actually touch those objects. The brain captures and retains physical sensations through touch, and can re-experience those sensations simply by seeing a visual image of them or imagining them.

Everyday challenges for developing and playing with our five senses

Try getting dressed, washing your hair and brushing your teeth with your eyes closed. When you have dinner with someone, try to communicate with your eyes instead of by talking. Smell flowers while you listen to music. Tap your fingers in time with the patter of rain. Observe the clouds while you make something out of clay. Take a different route to work or school for a week. When you eat, hold your fork in your other hand. Shop at a different store or bakery.

Creative visualisation

Connecting your senses with what you are trying to create can be extremely effective. Try using your five senses to visualise the final solution to your creative challenge. What does it look like? How does it feel to the touch? What does it sound like? What does it smell like? What does it taste like? The more emotionally connected you are to your creative challenge, the more likely you are to discover a creative solution.

Sixth sense

I can see dead people...

In neuroscience, 'proprioception' is frequently referred to as the sixth sense. It is responsible for registering the position, movement and posture of the body in space, and re-transmitting that information to the brain. However, it often occurs on an unconscious level – for example, when we maintain or adjust our balance. The somatosensory system, along with its proprioceptors, is responsible for measuring how muscle length, tension and pressure relate to the position of the body. This takes place in our ligaments, tendons, muscles, joints and skin. The proprioceptors transmit the information to the brain, which can make decisions like commanding the muscles to change position or stop moving. When we drink alcohol or take other drugs, this system becomes distorted or defective. That's why when a police officer asks us to stand on one leg, touch our nose with our index finger or walk in a straight line, we can't.

May I smell your underarms?

Other scientists consider the sixth sense to be the vomeronasal organ or VNO, which is located inside the nose and has the power to detect certain chemical signals transmitted by other people. Those signals are the hormones known as pheromones. Although these molecules, along with the VNO, have been studied in many animals, including insects, rats and monkeys, there is still some controversy about whether human VNO is functional or not. Pheromones trigger a huge variety of hormonal changes and instinctual behaviour such as the reproductive urge or aggressiveness. This has led to some manufacturers creating a range of perfumes that stimulate sexual attraction because they claim to contain human pheromones (the so-called sensual scents that have brand names like Realm, Desire 22 and Pheromone 10X).

A study carried out at the University of Chicago produced the strongest evidence that human pheromones exist. A group of young women were asked to smell cotton wool pads that contained underarm secretions from other young women. Within a short time their menstrual cycles became synchronised with those of their donors. Current thinking is that human pheromones might influence our behaviour in some unconscious part of our brain. However, the conscious part, through our senses, education and culture, exercises much greater control over us. In other words, smelling someone's pheromones, whether natural or synthetic, won't compel us to want to have sex with or attack that person, as happens with some animals.

Pheromones are produced in the apocrine glands, which are present in exposed areas of the skin, where they are responsible for secreting substances that destroy potentially harmful bacteria. They become active in puberty and are chiefly situated in the underarms, the nipples (of both sexes), the genital area, the area surrounding the lips, the eyelids and in the outer ear. The first four of these areas are associated with the growth of body hair during puberty, which makes sense because puberty is the time when we start to become interested in sex. What's more, those areas where there is hair growth are extremely efficient at giving off smells through evaporation. Perhaps we have discovered the purpose of underarms: to secrete pheromones. They are located at nose level and we constantly move our arms about so the other can 'smell us'. Of course we aren't machines that surrender to smells, but it is quite likely that our behaviour is guided by a harmonious mixture of pheromones and intellect.

I told you there was a biological explanation!

Finally, everyone is talking about it: women's sixth sense, commonly known as female intuition. This has nothing to do with pheromones or proprioception. It is due to the fact that women are better than men at perceiving when someone's body language contradicts what they are saying. In a study carried out at Harvard, a group of men and women were shown silent film clips depicting different situations. Only forty-two percent of men were able to decipher what was going on compared to eighty-seven percent of women. This ability becomes even more accentuated in mothers, who have to communicate with their children very early on, before they learn to speak. However, in the Harvard experiment, men who were social workers, nurses or artists, and homosexuals, scored the same as women. Some scientists think that women's elevated levels of oestrogen partially explain their ability to detect details in their environment and to notice changes.

One fascinating, and occasionally dangerous, aspect of our body language and facial expressions is that we are seldom aware of how our posture, movements and gestures can say one thing while our voice says another. This is where women score higher than men so, men, beware of what you say! Women are more sensitive to facial expressions, and better able to detect someone's state of mind or mood simply by looking in their eyes. Several studies of primary school children showed that, on average, girls make more eye contact than their male classmates. In another recent study, using nuclear MRI, it was discovered that there are between fourteen and sixteen areas in women's brains devoted to evaluating other people's behaviour, compared to four to six percent in men. This might explain why women think that men don't talk much, and why men think that women never stop talking. What's more, women can talk about two, three or four different subjects simultaneously, changing the inflection of their voice as many as five times when they want to emphasise something or change the subject. We men are only capable of detecting three out of those five tones, which explains why we often can't follow what they are saying. Don't get angry, girls!

On average, women use about fifteen thousand words a day while men only use around seven thousand. A study carried out in 2003 on university students showed that female students took twice as long to end a conversation on instant messaging than their male counterparts, and that they used many more pictorial as well as punctuation emoticons, the most obvious one of course being :-). According to the anthropologist Ray Birdwhistell, a pioneer of non-verbal communication, humans are capable of understanding around two hundred and fifty thousand facial expressions. Unbelievable.

I can hear colours

If I were to show you some objects that are rounded and some others that are sharp or serrated and ask you to name them using the words 'kiki' and 'bouba', I am sure you would decide to call the rounded ones 'bouba' and the serrated ones 'kiki'. This is what is known as mild synaesthesia, where words that have a curvy sound are associated with rounded or curved shapes. Synaesthesia is a condition that occurs when your senses overlap, as if the circuits and wires in the brain were crossed: people who say they see colours when they listen to music (like the painter Vasily Kandinsky) or vice versa, as well as other interesting combinations. It has been estimated that one out of every twenty thousand people suffers from synaesthesia. However, the number is probably higher because many sufferers aren't aware that they have a rare condition. In a recent study of one thousand seven hundred people, one out of every twenty-three had a degree of synaesthesia. Some experts associate synaesthesia with creativity.

ATTENTION

Pay attention, I said

'So many of our dreams at first seem impossible, then they seem improbable, and then, when we summon the will, they soon become inevitable.'

Christopher Reeve

In order to solve our challenge creatively, we must be ATTENTIVE to what is in front of us and develop the ability to focus on our objective. We work an average of eight hours a day, forty-eight weeks a year. We check our emails every five minutes (twenty-four thousand times a year!) to see if we have new messages (not to read them and reply). It takes on average ten seconds to do that and then go back to concentrating on what we were doing. Some people say it takes them between thirty seconds and three minutes! We spend 66.6 hours a year simply checking if we have an email.

Continued

Ask yourself: do you find it hard to focus on what you are doing because you are constantly looking beyond what you have in front of you? Write a list of ways you can minimise those distractions (by switching off your mobile, not turning on your computer, not opening your email, restricting the hours when you can make calls or send texts, creating quiet spaces for yourself, etc.)

Imagine the alphabet in capital letters. Can you say how many of the letters have curved lines? Pay attention to how you think about this. Before seeing whether a letter has curved lines or not, each letter will appear in your mind. You will see how they appear in sequence: first A, then B, then C, etc., rather than spontaneously. Our thought is linear because it's impossible for us to pay close attention to everything at once. Our attention is usually scattered, and it is our 'intention' that decides what we decide to focus on out of everything around us, all our possible experiences.

Alphabetic sources

Write down the letters A–Z on the left-hand side of a sheet of paper.

Next to each letter, write down the name of a famous person that begins with that letter. For example, a: Alfred the Great, b: Boris Becker, etc.

Imagine how those people would confront your creative challenge. Adapt or associate.

This intention allows you to achieve your goal. Intention helps you pay attention to those things your brain considers truly important, your goals. The decision your intention makes filters out your perceptions enabling you to invest a certain amount of time and attention in a given situation. During that period, the information you receive from the experience acquires meaning and leads you to act in a particular way. If you look up at the clouds with the intention of seeing a shape, say of a cow or a balloon, I guarantee that if you try hard enough, you will find a cow or a balloon in the clouds. The shape of the clouds hasn't changed and neither have your eyes. The only thing that has changed is your intention, and that intention is what enables your mind to find what it is looking for. Your consciousness will arrange and rearrange the clouds until your mind finds the cow or the balloon.

Our intention tells us to what and where to pay attention. Lots of studies show that the more attention our brain gives to a particular stimulus, the more complex the information we are able to memorise and retain. It's a sure thing: *the more attentive we are, the better we learn.* With the advent of PowerPoint and other presentations used in all kinds of events, it is useful to know that within twenty minutes people, or rather their brains, will no longer be paying attention. If keeping people's interest in a class or seminar were a business, we would fail eighty percent of the time. We still don't know why attention span is so short, but it is essential to find ways of making people sit up and listen in order to convey your message efficiently. Messages or any type of stimuli that catch our attention do so because they connect to our interest, our memory and our understanding of a given subject.

We still don't understand exactly why, but it is clear that there is a close relationship between our interest in specific things and what we pay attention to. Our brain is constantly scanning stimuli, and when it finds something that interests us, our attention will instantly home in on it. Professionals working in advertising are convinced that attention can also generate interest. When they confront us with a new, unusual, unpredictable or distinctive stimulus, they are wielding a powerful tool with which to draw our attention and thus rouse our interest. In our everyday lives, we use previous experience (memory) in order to know what to pay attention to.

Focus your attention

It is essential to have a clear idea of what your creative challenge is before generating ideas. Your challenge requires maximum attention.

Developing your attention

Choose a random colour and spend the whole day looking for that colour in everything you see.

Spend five minutes writing down all the improvements that could be made to the place where you find yourself (train, room, office, park, etc.), from the guardrail round the sandpit to the fan on the ceiling.

Spend five minutes inventing names for non-alcoholic drinks that enhance athletic performance (remember always to write everything down). The names should be suggestive, adventurous, amusing, etc.

Emotionally charged events

Although the biology behind conscious attention is far from being understood, one thing is for sure: *emotions draw our attention*. When we experience an event that is emotionally charged, we remember it in more detail and for longer than we would a more neutral one. Your first kiss, the death of a loved one, your last day at school, an accident, a family Christmas, etc. Some events are charged with emotions specific to individuals, others are universal and we experience them in more or less the same way; they are written in our DNA. For example, danger or energy sources (food). No matter where you live or who you are, you will always pay great attention to such stimuli: can I eat it? Can it eat me? Can I breed with him/her? Will he/she want to breed with me? Have I seen this before? If our ancestors hadn't been able to remember accurately the dangers of their environment (remember the leopards?) and where to get food, water and shelter, they wouldn't have survived to pass on their genes. As we already saw, our brain contains systems that specifically look for opportunities to breed and to perceive the dangers around us. This is why we pay special attention to events like muggings and accidents.

The brain recalls the emotional components of an event more precisely than any other detail or aspect of it, i.e. the brain processes meaning before details. Words organised logically in an ordered structure are forty percent easier to remember than the same words arranged arbitrarily. If we can spot the connection between one word and another, we will remember the details more easily. *Meaning before details.*

A widespread myth about attention is that some people, mainly women, are capable of multitasking, i.e. they can pay attention to several things at once. This is false because the brain naturally focuses on one thing at a time, in sequence, as we saw in the exercise on p. 138. Obviously we can do things like walking, reading and listening to music simultaneously. But it's impossible to pay attention properly to more than two activities at once without a deficit in understanding, efficiency, performance, etc. Studies show that when someone attempts to perform several tasks simultaneously, paying attention to each one, they will often interrupt an activity themselves, because they become absorbed in a previous task. It is estimated that they take twice as long to perform each task and make twice as many mistakes. The most we can say about these 'multi-taskers' is that they have excellent memories, and can therefore pay attention to lots of different things, one at a time. A classic example is talking on a mobile or texting while driving. We now know that it takes the brain fractions of a second to switch from one task to another. A person talking on a mobile takes half a second longer to apply the brakes in an emergency stop. During that half second a car travelling at seventy miles an hour will have travelled fifteen yards. People talking on the phone miss more than fifty percent of road signs seen by attentive drivers.

When you find yourself attempting to do more than one thing at a time, calm down and try to do just one. When you need to concentrate, rid yourself of all possible outside distractions.

> Reduce the likelihood of inner distractions by clearing your thoughts before addressing your challenge.

Finally, we should be aware that one of the classic errors in communication is to pass on too much information without allowing enough time for people to understand and make connections – filling them with knowledge without giving them time to digest it. This often happens because experts know their subject so well and they forget that the majority of their audience are novices. Expertise isn't a guarantee of good communication or teaching skills. Many of the professors whose lectures I was lucky enough to attend at Harvard weren't skilled communicators, a fact that was reflected in the end of semester lecturer surveys.

In short: after between ten and twenty minutes of a talk, lecture or speech, most people are already 'daydreaming'. A very effective way of catching people's attention is to relate emotionally charged stories or events that will refuel their neuronal connections.

Stories

Imagine that you are in a distant country. Write a brief story describing the place. Fill it with emotion. How would you solve your creative challenge there? Re-read it and look for associations and clues for your current challenge.

Imagine you are living in a different period of history. Write down what you would do to solve your creative challenge. Re-read it and look for associations and clues for your current challenge.

To sum up: the brain processes meaning before details. Confronted with information, it offers us the general ideas before attending to each separate detail. A bit like a glass of water in the desert for the message receptors. Multitasking stimulates us, but the brain is incapable of it. When we try to do too many things at once, we make more mistakes and spend more time on the tasks in hand. A good idea is to create a 'no-interruption zone' during the day, and you will see how much more efficiently you perform tasks. No interruptions means switching off your mobile, not putting it on vibrate.

Move one line to correct this erroneous sum.

IV = III + III

Easy, isn't it? Up to ninety percent of brain-damaged patients succeed in moving the 'I' from the left to the right side of the 'V' so that it reads VI = III + III

Here is a more difficult challenge to resolve by moving one line.

III = III + III

In this case, only forty-three percent of 'normal' people succeed in solving it. Most stare at the roman numerals for a few minutes and then give up. However, eighty-two percent of patients who have difficulty focusing their attention are able to solve it. The equation is a simple tautology (III + III + III). We aren't used to seeing arithmetic operators in an equation (+, −, =) and so we focus on the numerals. Sometimes forcing ourselves to focus on a problem doesn't help us to solve it; we have to be able to look at it from different perspectives.

If we want to build our muscles, we do weight lifting. In response to the stimulus (weights), some of our genes will be activated to produce more proteins in order to fuel muscle growth. Without our interaction with the weights, that activation wouldn't occur.

Something similar happens during the thought process. To think in an unconventional way and produce creative ideas we need to use intention. That intention (to see cows in cloud formations) encourages the activation of certain genes that produce new neurotransmitters. These in turn increase the number of connections between neurons. The more unusual, subtle connections the brain makes, the more likely we are to experience fresh insights. In addition, the more frequently we practise this, the more active and creative our brain becomes. Using intentionality energises our brain, which enables it to generate more new ideas.

I recommend that you become highly conscious of what you really want, so that you are better able to ignite and activate your creative potential.

A map of your intentions

Write down on a board or a sheet of paper (your map) the actual intention of your challenge. Surround it with images, articles and sentences from magazines or other sources relating to your aim. These intentions will do a lot to stimulate your brain.

'When there's no wind, row.'

Latin Proverb

Intentional insights

Here is one of those riddles that require an insight to find the solution: you are an oncologist and you have a patient with a malignant tumour in their stomach. The tumour is inoperable, but if it isn't removed the patient will die. A machine exists with a ray powerful enough to destroy it, but unfortunately the healthy tissue it penetrates to reach the tumour will also be destroyed. If you lower the intensity of the ray, the tissue will be unharmed, but the tumour won't be destroyed. Your creative challenge is: how do you use the rays to destroy the tumour without harming the healthy tissue?

Ninety-seven percent of people conclude that the problem is insoluble. But let's see what happens if I tell you the following story. At the centre of a country stands a castle. Lots of small roads, like the spokes of a wheel, lead to and from the castle and they are mined. A general wants to capture the castle with his army, but at the same time he doesn't want his soldiers and the surrounding villages to be blown up. Obviously the general can't make the entire army attack the castle using only one road. On the other hand, if he is to capture the castle he will need all his soldiers. So, he divides his army into small groups, which he positions at equal distances on the various roads that converge on the castle. The soldiers attack at the same time and capture the castle.

Now can you solve the riddle about the tumour? Seventy percent of people manage to solve it after hearing the story about the castle. Understanding how the two stories are related generates a moment of revelation, an insight. The answer arises from the analogy. The doctor can set up ten machines with separate rays, adjusting the intensity of each ray to ten percent of what is needed to destroy the tumour. When aimed at the tumour, the ten rays will destroy it without harming the healthy tissue. The crucial element here is the intention with which we absorb information, concepts or ideas that may appear irrelevant. Rather than focus on the details of the problem (tumours, rays), we have to free our minds to search for remote ideas and analogies that enable us to find solutions. If you were among the seventy percent who solved the riddle after hearing the military story, you have just experienced an insight!

True creatives

Although there are many useful techniques for developing and enhancing creativity, it is fair to say that there is no magic recipe we can follow that makes us creative. However, there are many studies of people whose daring creative leaps have changed paradigms, and they can provide interesting insights. We are talking about people who have contributed significantly to changing or enhancing their field of expertise.

As humans we try to categorise everything; we feel more at ease when we know the whys and wherefores of things. Creativity experts conducted a study of ninety-six people considered by their peers to be highly creative. Among them are historians, composers, philosophers, critics, poets, architects, writers, biologists, doctors, chemists, physicists, astronomers, psychologists, social scientists, political activists, entrepreneurs, philanthropists, inventors, and they all have one thing in common: they have enormous *physical stamina*, although they are often calm, almost serene. *They work incredibly long hours* with a high level of concentration, and yet they have the sensation of feeling fresh and *excited* about what they are doing, in other words they aren't necessarily hyperactive. They are alert, murmuring to themselves in their heads. Something is always going on in their head, although they often relax too, and they sleep a lot. They are in control of their energy: they don't need deadlines or bosses to make them work and, if necessary, they can focus instantly, recharge their batteries and carry on. Another characteristic paradox is that they achieve a *combination of playfulness and discipline*, of responsibility and irresponsibility, a light-hearted attitude. At the same time they are tenacious, and have no illusions about the need to work hard for sustained periods in order for a new idea or insight to arise in their minds that will overcome the obstacles all creative people inevitably encounter. There is a popular myth that musicians, writers, poets and painters have vivid fantasy lives and prolific imaginations while scientists, politicians and entrepreneurs are more down to earth. This may apply to the everyday tasks they perform, but where starting a creative enterprise is concerned, a painter can be as down to earth as a physicist, and a physicist can have as many flights of fancy as a painter.

Other studies of hyper-creative individuals show that they can be extremely extrovert one minute and introvert the next; sometimes they are communicative and other times they are content to sit quietly and watch the world go by. They are also remarkably modest and proud at the same time, and most of the time they are so focused on current challenges or future projects that whatever they have achieved in the past is no longer important. *They enjoy the process far more than the results.* They are frequently seen as rebellious and independent, and yet they couldn't possibly be different without first having studied and learned about the discipline to which they are applying their creativity. They unite the traditional and conservative with the rebellious. Tradition seldom leads to change, but by taking certain risks, highly creative people break with the safety of those traditions, which is necessary for insights to occur. Basically, they are all *passionate about their work*, they love what they do and without that passion they lose interest, and where there is little interest there are fewer chances of being creative. *Creativity requires intention.*

Possibly the single most important quality which creative people possess is their capacity to enjoy the creative process itself, not as a means to an end. **Enjoyment** is enormously important for people who work creatively.

Remember: whether or not you share the above characteristics, attitudes or ways of responding to different stimuli, the techniques in this book will help you to enhance your creative thinking.

Stop reading for a moment and observe three or four objects next to you. How might you use those objects or the associations they produce to improve this book?

The faster your mind focuses on the problem it wants to solve, the more quickly you will come up with creative solutions.

Continued

Write down the three main priorities (3P) in your life that require creativity. When you are travelling, listening to music, reading or chatting with a stranger, look for connections to your 3Ps. As if you were out hunting for things that relate to your priorities. You needn't associate your 3Ps urgently; they aren't dreams or ambitions, or a list of projects. They are open, conceptual loops through which you are continuing on your quest for insights.

Curious energy

Creativity, or being more creative in your life, won't necessarily bring you fame or fortune. But it will make your everyday experiences more intense, more enjoyable, and they will bring you a feeling of reward. When we live creatively, boredom tends to evaporate. Each moment holds the promise of something fresh, new, different. These discoveries may not enrich the world at large, but besides enhancing our own experience, living creatively also brings us closer to the evolutionary process. As we have already seen, we all have the potential in our minds to live or pursue a more creative life. And yet, everyday obstacles prevent us from attaining our full potential. Many of us are tired because too many demands are made on us during the day. We have trouble mustering the energy required to be creative. Some of us are easily distracted and find it hard to learn new things, because our energy channels are already in use. Another obstacle is laziness or the lack of discipline required to control the energy we could use to be more creative. Finally, many of us don't know how to use the energy we have.

To be able to use our energy in the creative process, we need spaces where we can focus our attention at different times during our day or week, which can inspire the new.

Most of our attention in life is focused on external needs: we can't expect someone holding down two jobs, or balancing a busy career and childcare to have the mental energy to be really creative. Even so, many of our obstacles are internal. When our main concern is to protect ourselves, most of our attention is focused on monitoring anything that might threaten our ego. We devote too much attention to highly personal, egocentric aims. We all need to take care of ourselves, to achieve or attempt to satisfy our needs, and yet for some that need is inflated to the point where they think of nothing else. When a person sees, thinks or acts in a way that relates solely to their own interest, they haven't enough attention or energy left to learn other things, and thus to be more open and more creative. It's difficult to be creative if you are hungry or cold, because you need all your energy to cover those basic needs. It's equally difficult for the rich and famous to be creative if all they do is struggle to obtain more wealth and fame.

In order to release our creative energy, we need to curb our constant search for goals. Our genes, on the one hand, and our cultural memes, on the other, have programmed us to pursue this endless quest. Let's use this newly released energy to explore the world around us. To achieve a more creative life *we need to use our attention to cultivate curiosity and interest*, to pay attention to things for the sake of the things themselves. This is what children do. Their curiosity is like a laser, permanently moving, focusing their interest on anything they see or touch. Creative adults quite often resemble children because their curiosity is always fresh. Even at ninety years old, some of them still derive great enjoyment from the new, the unusual, the unknown.

Advice for those who aren't very curious or aren't in the habit of becoming interested in new things

Try to be surprised by something every day. It might be something you see, hear or read. For example, stop looking at parked cars the way you usually do and look at them in a different way, try a new dish at a restaurant, really listen to a colleague at work. Don't assume you know all about something, or even if you do, try to put that out of your mind; as if you were looking at it for the first time. Experience things for what they are and not for what we think they are. Try to surprise someone, tell him or her something different, unexpected, give an opinion you would never normally dare express, ask a question that is atypical for you, break the routine of your activities by inviting him or her to a restaurant, theatre or museum, where neither of you have been before.

Write down each day what surprised you and how you surprised someone. After a few weeks, read back over what you did, how you surprised someone, etc. You will discover different patterns, things that interest you more than others, possibly a new subject you would like to study more deeply.

If something arouses your interest, however trivial, pursue it, explore it, anything that grabs your attention, whether it's a song, an idea or a restaurant. We are often too busy to explore the things that interest us. We may feel they aren't really our thing, they aren't very important, we have no time; never mind, explore it anyway. Your world is your time, your business and your work.

All children are curious, and that curiosity provides them with the energy and interest to be more creative. As we have already seen, this ability atrophies during childhood, especially when we start school. And yet we can gradually rekindle that curiosity and become, or rather go back to being, naturally more curious. Curiosity gives you more opportunities to be creative.

Break your routine

Routine is often the enemy of creativity.

Schedule changes into your daily routine. Make a list of things you do out of habit, always in the same way. Generally speaking, you will find some of the things on your list make your life easier enabling you to do them almost without thinking.

Identify one thing on your list that you do purely out of habit.

Try to modify how you do it that day, week, or month.

For example, take a different route to work or school, change the hours you sleep or work, switch radio stations, read a different newspaper, make new friends, drink fruit juice instead of tea, try a new restaurant, alternate showers and baths, watch a different TV programme, etc.

Curiosity revisited

'Curiosity is the most powerful thing we own.'

James Cameron

'Sometimes the questions are complicated and the answers are simple.'

Doctor Seuss

Every morning, set yourself a very specific goal. Something, no matter how big or small, which the evening before makes you look forward to getting up.

Most of us don't feel that our actions have much meaning. A lot of us live on automatic pilot. But if you put your mind to it, you will discover at least one thing every day for which it is worth getting up in the morning. This could be a new acquaintance, a gift you buy for someone special, planting a tree, tidying your desk, writing a letter, wearing a new item of clothing, etc. After you have kept this up for a while, you will find yourself looking forward to each new day. Getting up will feel like a privilege instead of an ordeal. Experience in a different way all those daily routines like brushing your teeth, having breakfast, getting dressed, washing, etc. The quality of our experience tends to improve, the more effort we put into it. **When we do something and we do it well, it becomes much more enjoyable**. Start changing the way you perform routine activities and you will start to enjoy them again.

Increase the complexity of the things you do. When you repeat the same activity every day, you will start to get bored unless you find new challenges or opportunities. Improve, expand or do everything better and better. The more you know about your activity, the more complex it will become, and the more you will enjoy it too. By doing all this, you will awaken your interest and learn how to be curious again. You will release your creative energy, which you must defend tooth and nail.

Be in control of your time. I realise this is difficult for a lot of us who work between eight and ten hours. I am talking about making small adjustments. They will enable you to have a bit more creative energy. Get up or go to bed earlier or later than usual, go to the park, catch a different bus, take a stroll before you start work, go down unfamiliar streets. I do this, and it works.

Let your everyday activities harmonise with your own daily rhythms. When do you feel at your best? When you eat? Sleep? On your way to work? You don't have to eat lunch at noon, why not eat a bit later? This is about identifying and reconciling as best you can the ideal pattern of our daily routines with our way of being. I realise that most of us have lots to do during the day and that some of those tasks can't be altered. But still, I assure you that time is far more flexible than we think. Just try it – you will see that you can make those small adjustments.

Spend time reflecting and relaxing. People who are successful and hard-working are like racing cars; they never stop. This makes them anxious, uneasy, always busy working and with an urgent need to be doing something all the time. Being busy all the time isn't good for creativity. It's important that you have the time during the day, the week, the year, to change down a gear. To take a fresh look at what you are doing and where you are going. These spaces won't appear by magic. Your boss or spouse won't create them for you, you have to do that yourself. They aren't a luxury; they are essential for your wellbeing. The owners or managers of some of the innovative companies I study and which I visit, insist that their employees take this time out. It doesn't come naturally, because they think there is 'never' time. Much of the creative and innovative success of these organisations comes from the moments of reflection and relaxation they impose on their employees. We have already seen that this is the best way to stimulate the appearance of creative insights in the brain.

Neither constant stress nor permanent monotony promotes creativity. You should alternate between periods of stress (a degree of stress can enhance performance) and periods of relaxation. Relaxation doesn't necessarily mean doing nothing; it can be relaxing to change your routines or daily chores.

Relax

Here are a few easy relaxation techniques for anyone who doesn't want to study or practise meditation: close your eyes, take a deep breath and count backwards from ten to one. Imagine a blue hot air balloon in the distance and keep looking at it. Fill that balloon with all your worries. Once you have done that, imagine the balloon has been untethered and is floating very slowly up into the air, drifting far into the distance. All you have to do is watch as the balloon disappears, carrying away all your concerns.

In 2009, Clayton Christensen, a professor at Harvard Business School, published a six-year study he had carried out on three thousand executives and five hundred innovative entrepreneurs. These were his two most important conclusions:

1) Five abilities distinguish the most creative people from others. **They are better at making associations** between seemingly unrelated concepts (conceptual blending). **They are curious about everything**, arriving at the heart of creativity (see the following technique). **They have enormous concentration and attention** (intention and attention) when observing what goes on in the world and imagining how it might be different. **They experiment without fear of failure**, amusing themselves until they find the best solution (enjoyment). **They seek out people who are different from them** to challenge their ideas and expand their horizons (perspectives).

2) Approximately eighty percent of our creativity can be learned and acquired. Incorporating into your daily routine techniques that are designed to develop your creativity (like those suggested in this book), you can increase your creative capacity anywhere from twenty to fifty percent.

Questions

Most of us were brought up not to challenge authority, in particular in the workplace, at school or in our families. That is why we often don't ask the right questions. In order to encourage a fresh, curious mind, you should make it part of your routine to question things constantly.

Continued

Why? Because it helps you to understand the way things are, challenge the status quo and challenge conventional wisdom.

Why is there always such a long queue to get into the cinema? Why do people wait until it rains to buy an umbrella? Why is it normal to work forty hours a week? Why is our business competitor outstripping us with that new product? Why don't they show my favourite TV programme more often?

What would happen if... ? This helps you to explore new possibilities and to imagine what the world would be like if you made some changes or developed a new idea.

What would happen if we charged a subscription for our product instead of a one-off fee? What would happen if the Stock Exchange went up by fifteen percent this year? What would happen if there was more of a police presence in the city? What would happen if we stopped having company meetings? What would happen if they reduced the legal age for drinking alcohol to fifteen?

Why not... ? This helps you to understand restrictions and make connections with the limiting factors that are blocking positive change.

Why aren't there more male nurses? Why don't the employees in our company share controversial ideas? Why don't we offer our customers a free car wash when they buy a car at our showroom?

The five whys that enable you to get to the root of the problem

1) Why do our customers prefer the potato chips sold by our competitors? Because they taste better.

2) Why do they taste better? Because they use better flavours than we do.

3) Why do they use better flavours? Because their chef is better than ours.

4) Why don't we hire a better chef? Because we never considered it important, so we have been stuck with the same mediocre chef for twenty years.

5) Why didn't we hire a new chef? Because no one wanted to put the question to our boss.

Astonishment report

Write a list of questions about everything that astonishes you in relation to your creative challenge. Read it and re-read it; you will doubtless find pointers that fuel your creativity.

Once you have identified your creative challenge, spend ten minutes every day for a month writing down all the questions you can think of about your challenge. As the days go by, your questions will change radically, giving you a deeper understanding of the subject and helping you to focus.

Who? What? Where? When? Why?

Think about your creative challenge.

Can you answer the above five questions in a precise and meaningful way?

If you are ready to put your solution into practice, start by asking yourself how.

Increasing your attention span

Training concentration, attention and awareness is essential to improving learning, creativity and stimulating the appearance of insights: in short, it increases our creativity. There are various techniques that can generate physiological and psychological changes in the body and mind. Many of these techniques are derived from thousand-year-old philosophies and ideas, and each is founded on relatively simple daily practice. These may be focusing the attention on something internal, such as our breathing or heartbeat, or on external sounds such as music, or an object. Some exercises incorporate both. I can confirm from personal experience that, to begin with, it takes considerable effort to train your mind to be more attentive. With practice, as with most learning, the effort diminishes and you start automatically to concentrate on the exercises. If you make yourself practise them daily, the results are remarkable. Needless to say, you must follow the advice of those instructing you.

A more western technique is known as 'active attentional training'. A lot of us train our attention without realising we are doing it, especially when we practise sport, outside activities, or hobbies. Examples of this kind of attention can be found in activities that are driven by novelty, speed and an intense, self-imposed state of effortless concentration – for example, hill running, where we have to pay attention to the terrain, constantly change speed and we never know what's behind the next tree or rock. And by deliberate repetition in a safe environment, where we can lower our guard because there is no need for us to change abruptly to adapt to the circumstances, we are flowing – for example running on a track or on a straight road. In both cases, a good physical workout also ensures that you are mentally training your attention. With time, these psychophysiological changes go beyond physical health and help us to attain a state of mental wellbeing that stimulates creativity. Those of us who play sport get a lot of good ideas while exercising.

We can also train our attention while sitting still. This is known as 'mindfulness'. The word comes from Buddhism and is used nowadays to designate a range of different things. For the purposes of our mental training and the aims of this book, I shall leave aside the spiritual aspect of mindfulness and refer only to the practical side. Mindfulness isn't the search for change. On the contrary it's about being who you are, having what you have, existing in the moment at every moment. Rather than focusing and excluding, it's about remaining calm, being attentive to something extremely small, such as the breath, and then gradually opening our senses to everything that is going on around us. The challenge of this practice is letting go of each new sensation or thought as it arises, allowing you to return to the breath and to the moment. Your initial response will probably be frustration when you can't control your attention, which is what happens to me when I start to think about the steak and chips I ate last night. However, you soon realise that it's all right, that it's normal for the mind to wander. You stop seeing it as something good or bad, and it becomes simply what it is: the way our mind works. Don't fight it, but cherish it, accept it and return to the breath.

Lastly, I would like to recommend you try transcendental meditation. It was Maharishi Mahesh Yogi who first introduced this technique more than fifty years ago. Today, it is thought that over five million people practise transcendental meditation daily. It is a form of meditation that uses mantras (sounds) based on the Vedic traditions and teachings. In transcendental meditation you have your own mantra, given to you by an instructor, and by repeating and focusing internally on that mantra, you attain a state of calm. In 1979, a study carried out by the creativity expert Ellis Paul Torrence showed that people who practised transcendental meditation were more creative when performing various tasks than the control group who didn't. What's more, there is strong evidence that practising TM improves mood and our ability to confront fear and doubt.

The practices of both mindfulness and transcendental meditation are supported by thousands of scientific publications. Even though I am open to everything, I am something of a sceptic where spirituality is concerned. I need a practice to work in my own life before I can believe in it and start recommending it to others.

EMOTIONS

Thrills and spills

Our emotional experience is associated with a network in the brain known as the limbic system, which detects the emotional connection to our thoughts, to objects, people and events. It tells you how you feel at every instant in relation to the world, determining and guiding your behaviour, often unconsciously. Without a complete limbic system, your brain wouldn't function properly. You would be able to wake up and get out of bed, but after that you would probably remain there, paralysed. We are making choices all the time. Of course we don't have the time or the energy to process infinite possible actions in a logical way. Should we have breakfast? What should we have for breakfast? Should we sleep more? All those small decisions entail much more than a simple rational process.

Well-known scientists Evian Gordon and Lea Williams developed a model called 'integrate', which proposes that everything we do in our lives is based on the brain's determination to minimise danger and maximise reward. It is the brain's organising principle. The limbic system registers all incoming information and tells us to which stimuli we must pay attention and how. It encourages us to approach stimuli that produce emotions like curiosity, happiness and joy, and avoid those that produce anxiety, sadness and fear. The stimuli we try to avoid are known as primary dangers: hunger, a tiger, an angry face, intense heat, etc. Those that help us to survive are primary *rewards*: food, money, sex, a familiar face, etc. In other words, the limbic system constantly registers and classifies stimuli (approach/avoid), and accordingly determines how we should behave.

Generally speaking, these decisions are unconscious and are taken a split second before we become aware of the action we already decided upon. The limbic system springs into action more forcefully when it perceives danger than when it senses reward, and also the response to a threat is much faster, longer lasting and more difficult to switch off: 'Sadness has no end; happiness does'.

If you are presenting your idea to someone, and they say at some point, 'yes, but...' you could try to instantly rephrase that as 'yes, and...'

When someone says to you, 'this isn't going to work', try to come up with three ways in which it will work.

If someone says to you, 'this can't be done', try to find three ways to do it.

Although everyone's limbic system is activated when confronted by certain situations, we all have our 'unique activation buttons' which are the result of personal experience we have stored and labelled as 'dangerous'. When the initial source of this experience, or something similar, reappears in your life, it triggers your response to danger, which is equal to the degree of danger it was labelled with originally. 'Once bitten, twice shy.'

Hyperactivation of the limbic system, whether as a result of real or imaginary dangers or rewards, can cause the brain to malfunction. This often happens without us realising it, and can even give us false sense of confidence. For example, when you experience fear, your adrenaline increases making you more focused, which in turn gives you more confidence to make decisions. But in fact, your decision-making ability is reduced. This hyperactivation can also deprive the prefrontal cortex of the energy it needs to function properly; there is less glucose and oxygen available to understand, decide, memorise, classify and inhibit thoughts – five of the everyday primordial functions of the prefrontal cortex. Recent studies have shown that the functioning of our prefrontal cortex can be compromised by the simple fact of perceiving an angry face instead of a smiley face at the end of an email. This shows how relatively easy it is to overload the limbic system, reducing the performance of the prefrontal cortex as well as inhibiting our ability to live and to understand what is happening in the moment; we tend to overreact to adverse situations, take fewer risks, look on the negative side of things and see connections between things where there are none. Commonly known as persecution complex.

The Disney Method

What did Disney do? Confronted with a creative challenge, he looked at it from three different angles, assumed three different roles, then connected those roles to his challenge.

Day 1. The Dreamer: let your imagination run free without worrying about how to implement any ideas that might arise.

Day 2. The Realist: bring your fantasies down to earth by attempting to see how you might put into practice what your imagination has created.

Day 3. The Spoiler: pose questions and look for the weak points in your idea.

Example: I am the manager of a group, and my creative challenge is: 'I want my staff to come to my office more frequently so that I can see how they are feeling and how they are working.'

Day 1. The Dreamer: we should install floating chairs in all the corridors so that staff can sit on them and they will instantly come to my office.

Day 2. The Realist: floating chairs haven't been invented yet, but if we got some comfortable chairs for my office, they might come in more often.

Day 3. The Spoiler: how much are these new chairs going to cost? What if all the employees decide they want the same chairs in their offices? What if they become so relaxed they stop listening to me? And so on...

Self-regulate

Many of us make the classic mistake of thinking that suppressing a feeling is the best way to keep calm under pressure. James Gross, a professor at Stanford University and an expert on emotion regulation, has outlined some of the strategies we can use to avoid emotional stress overload:

1) **Situation selection**: if you are no good at presenting your project to your boss or a client, you can choose not to do so.

2) **Situation modification**: if you have no choice but to present your project to your boss, modify the situation in some way (for example, be better prepared).

3) **Response modulation**: while presenting your idea to your boss, try to deflect your anxiety, tension and nerves. You will get nervous, you can't avoid that, but you will be less affected because you are aware of it.

These three choices work well, but only if those emotions haven't already manifested themselves. What happens if you are already experiencing them? In this case you have two choices: 1) *Express your emotions*: if you are sad, cry the way a child would (obviously this isn't possible in all social situations). 2) *Cognitive change*: even in the middle of an emotional predicament, you can still rethink things, 'label' or 'reformulate' your emotions, i.e. change your interpretation of what is happening.

Doctor Gross found that people who attempted to suppress negative emotions failed. Trying 'not to feel' something is not only difficult but can be counterproductive. If you try to suppress an emotion in the presence of another, his or her blood pressure will increase. The observer expects to see an emotion, but none is forthcoming. In other words, suppressing emotions literally makes the person next to you feel uncomfortable.

Labelling emotions. Professor Matthew Lieberman discovered through the use of an MRI scanner that the level of activity in the amygdala of participants decreased when they described or labelled an emotion. They felt less emotionally stressed. Labelling what you feel activates a region in the brain responsible for inhibiting or slowing thoughts: cogitate less and you feel less stressed. This also shows that it is wrong to assume that talking about emotions makes things worse. On the contrary, describing an emotion in one or two words helps to diminish it. With time, this practice, which at first is conscious and intentional, will become habitual, almost natural. The brain starts to rewire itself in order to become more effective at dealing with its emotions.

Reformulating an emotion. There are four different techniques, depending on the situation. 1) *Reinterpret* an event or situation. As we reinterpret, we decide whether the event is threatening or not. 2) *Normalise*. Describe in a conscious way the different emotions you are going to experience during a change in your life in order to reduce the threat. Starting a new job will make me anxious at first, then unsure of myself, then nostalgic, etc. 3) *Reorganise the information*. Change the list of priorities in your head. If your job is high on your list and suddenly you have a child, your child will probably come first now. In this way negative emotions about your work cause you less stress. 4) *Reposition yourself*. This entails putting yourself in another's shoes in order to see things from a different perspective. We generally have fixed ideas about what happens around us and to us, and so this technique is the most difficult, because it implies being able to abandon our fixed ideas in different situations.

Certainly any of these reformulation techniques is extremely effective in helping to control our emotions and prevent our limbic system from becoming hyperactivated. Many studies show that people who practise them live more contented lives. Start reformulating!

Emotion vs. feelings

If we stop to reflect for a moment about the quality and meaning of our existence, we will come to the conclusion that emotions are the most essential part of our mental life. Emotions make life worth living, and sometimes, sadly, they also bring it to an end. That's why so many disciplines are concerned with these phenomena, from philosophy to neurology, psychology, evolutionary biology and even economics.

Since the time of the Ancient Greeks, we humans have been inclined to separate reason from passion, thought from feeling, and cognition from emotion. Plato maintained that passion, desires and fears prevent us from thinking. Even our legal systems treat crimes of passion differently from other crimes, such as those involving premeditation. Emotion, then, could be considered the most personal and sometimes idiosyncratic human phenomenon. It expresses, in a very individual way, how we see the world, and can determine our subjective wellbeing.

Emotions seem like conscious feelings, but in fact they are physiological responses to different stimuli. As we have already seen, they were designed to make us avoid situations of fear and approach those that offer a promise of reward or satisfaction. Emotions are generated continuously, and most of the time we are unaware of them. There is a sort of two-way traffic in our brain between the limbic system and the prefrontal cortex, as reason and emotion try in some way to converse. These connections mean that we experience many of our emotions in a conscious way. But also, because it is a two-way process, our conscious thoughts can, and do, affect our emotions. When we say we 'are thinking too much' about something, it is a sign that our thoughts are impinging on our feelings. Taken to an extreme, this situation can lead some people to have a panic attack. Each of our emotions is produced by a special network in different regions of the brain, including the hypothalamus and the pituitary gland. The latter control the production of hormones, which generate physical responses such as increased heart rate or muscle contractions.

Throughout evolutionary history, the limbic system, which generates emotional behaviour, has to a large extent been preserved in many very different species. All these species, including our own, need to fulfil certain biological imperatives to survive on the planet and pass on their genes to successive generations. At the very least we need to find food, protect ourselves from the environment and procreate. This applies to insects, worms, fish, rats and frogs as well as to people. All these animals or species are equipped with neural systems designed to achieve those aims. And the vertebrates among us (fish, reptiles, birds and mammals) also have neural systems that are responsible for emotional behaviour.

As mentioned above, emotional responses are largely unconscious. Freud was right when he said that conscious awareness is only the tip of the mental iceberg. We think of emotions as a conscious *experience*. And yet, when we examine emotion in the brain, we see that conscious emotional experience is only part of the system that produces it, and not necessarily an important function. For example, from the point of view of a person in love, feeling is the important thing. But for someone attempting to understand what love is, why it happens, where it comes from and why some people are more able to give and receive it than others, the actual feeling of love doesn't necessarily mean much, it may not be an integral or important part of the brain's emotional system.

In short, our emotions seem to have an obvious and at once mysterious quality; they are perhaps the part of our brain about which we know and understand the most, and yet, we often experience them without really knowing why they exist or where they come from. They can appear slowly or all at once, they can be painfully obvious or rather obscure. We can't understand why we so often wake up in a bad mood in the mornings. Our emotions may be at the centre of who we are, but they often seem to have an agenda of their own; they come and go, make us feel things, and we are none the wiser. It is certainly almost impossible to imagine a life without emotions. We live for our emotions, and we strive to create situations where we experience moments of joy and happiness, and, of course, avoid feelings of anxiety, sorrow, disappointment or distress.

Extreme opposites

Reflect about and write down what your creative challenge is.

Write down what would happen if you had all the resources in the world: money, time, people, machines, anything you like.

Think about what would happen if you had no resources, and write down what you would do in that situation.

Try combining them to see what happens.

For example:

Creative challenge: to arrive at work earlier.

Unlimited resources: I go there by helicopter and land on the roof of my office building.

No resources: I have to walk and therefore leave home two hours before I am due at work.

Combined: ....

Scientists disagree over a universal definition of the emotions. There are many different ways of defining or characterising the emotions, which may or may not be mutually exclusive. A simple way of describing emotions is to consider them as bodily responses arising from reward and punishment. Reward clearly has a positive connotation, and represents everything which people, and sometimes animals, continually strive to obtain. Punishment, on the other hand, represents something worth avoiding. It is only when we become conscious of our emotions that we experience what we call feelings. The recognition of our emotions is an essential aspect of our awareness. Some scientists maintain that emotions are simply responses that have evolved as part of our struggle to survive in the world. Others describe emotions as mental states resulting from our ability to register what is happening around us. Still others consider them social constructions. Ultimately, when it comes to emotions we all think we know what we are talking about, and yet they aren't so easy to define. A common way of classifying emotions is through the dimensional theory of valence (pleasantness or unpleasantness) and arousal (activated or non-activated), which depends on the intensity of the emotion. In modern society, people experience the majority of their emotions (guilt, shame, appreciation, jealousy) within a social context. The most important thing about **emotions** (a fact few people know) is that they all lead to action; **they dictate our behaviour**.

Doctor Ledoux revealed in the nineties that the amygdala is the guardian of the emotions in the brain. It has the ability to retain in its memory the various emotions we experience throughout our lives, without us being aware we are doing it. The direct, rapid connection between the thalamus and the amygdala enables the amygdala to receive instantaneously all the signals processed by the senses. This immediacy allows the amygdala to initiate certain responses before the prefrontal cortex has understood or analysed all the information. In other words, while the prefrontal cortex is still registering our emotions, the amygdala receives all the stimuli via a kind of super highway, generating responses that are almost instantaneous and automatic, such as laughing, fighting, running, crying. A split second later, that information reaches the prefrontal cortex, where is it evaluated in a more subtle way, in its proper context, so that a rational plan of action can be devised. If the evaluation made by the prefrontal cortex coincides with the instantaneous responses triggered by the amygdala, then the body will continue with them. If, however, after rational analysis a different response seems more appropriate (for example verbal rather than physical), then the prefrontal cortex will send messages to the hypothalamus to calm the situation, i.e. to shut down the amygdala.

Various experiments, carried out in 2004, established that most sensations of fear and anger are produced in the amygdala. The amygdala generates the typical fight or flight responses to fear, which often occur when we find ourselves in a life or death situation and our instinct for survival overrides our reason. If we flee when we are being mugged, we aren't acting very rationally because the mugger might shoot us. The amygdala is also wired in such a way that we feel 'natural' fear when confronted with certain stimuli: for example when a bird, a spider or a snake come close to us. Some emotions seem to be hard-wired into us from birth, and are apparent when we see babies laugh and cry soon after being born. Others appear to be learned, like guilt, which requires social conditioning through negative feedback.

Most scientists acknowledge the existence of between four and six basic emotions: fear, anger, sadness, happiness, surprise and disgust – the last two were added by the neuroscientist Antonio Damasio. Emotions also enhance memory. Apparently, memories are recorded in different ways depending on whether they had an emotional content or not: simple memories or recollections without any emotional content are stored in the hippocampus, while those with emotional content are mainly processed by the amygdala.

A theory developed a few years ago, at the University of Illinois, suggests that each of our brains has an emotional set point, a median or central point that measures our basic mood, our basic level of sadness, happiness, and so on. Certain events will push those points up or down, but often we return to our 'basic setting'. Generally speaking, people with more negative emotional states are pessimistic, anxiety-ridden, and try to avoid others, whereas those who enjoy positive emotional states are more active, extroverted and confident. Some scans reveal that those two groups of individuals respond differently when confronted with other people's emotions. For example, images of scary-looking people provoke much stronger responses in the amygdala of pessimistic people, while photographs of people smiling produce stronger responses in the amygdala of optimistic people.

As we are permanently evolving and progressing, it is possible for us to predict the kinds of changes that might occur in the human brain by observing how the brains of other species evolve. We now know that the amygdala influences the prefrontal cortex more than the cortex influences the amygdala. That is why, at certain moments, our emotions override our thoughts. If we look at mammals, the neural pathways from the amygdala to the prefrontal cortex are much more developed than those from the cortex to the amygdala. We all know how easy it is for thoughts to trigger emotions, and, you guessed right, they do so by activating the amygdala. We also know that thoughts aren't very effective in silencing our emotions, in shutting down the amygdala; telling ourselves we should be less anxious or depressed doesn't make that happen.

In primates the cortical connections between the prefrontal cortex and the amygdala are more numerous than in any other type of mammal, suggesting that these connections might continue to expand, giving the prefrontal cortex greater control over the amygdala. If that were to happen, future humans might be able to control their emotions better. If these new neural pathways were to reach a state of equilibrium, the dilemma between thought and emotion, between reason and passion might be resolved through a more harmonious integration. In other words, with an increase in connectivity between the prefrontal cortex and the amygdala, cognition and emotion might start working together, and not as separate systems the way they do now.

Changing one word

Years ago, Toyota suggested to its employees that they think up ways of being more productive. The management received few responses. After a while, they reformulated the question: how could employees make their jobs easier? The management was inundated with new ideas.

Tweaking a question can make a big difference.

Sometimes, changing a single word or the word order of a creative challenge can stimulate your imagination, adding different layers of meaning.

Define your challenge.

Identify key words and change them at least five times. It is always easier to change the verb. For example, my creative challenge is how can I work less?

Change one word: How can I travel less, how can I eat less, how can I sleep less, etc.

Write down new ideas that arise from changing one word.

Associate those ideas with your original challenge.

Two words

Write down the essence of your challenge in two words.

For example, if your challenge is 'how can I improve sales of my ice cream', the two key words are 'sales' and 'ice cream'.

Separate your challenge into two components: sales and ice cream.

Choose two attributes from each of those components. For example: retail sales online and offline; creaminess and flavours.

Choose two attributes from each original attribute.

Online: via email or website. Offline: pay the sales assistant or the checkout staff.

Creamy: thick and sweet. Flavour: fruity or chocolaty.

You can go on splitting these attributes into two until you feel you have enough new material to start working with. By doing this you break your challenge down into separate parts, and you discover fresh material that was or is part of something else. Then you try to stick the parts back together in an original way.

When you feel sad, your thoughts aren't the same as when you feel contented. When you feel rich and successful, your thoughts are also very different than when you feel poor and a failure. The same applies when you feel creative; your ideas are different than when you feel you aren't creative. Imagine that you are driving a car and the petrol gauge starts flashing to warn you that the tank is almost empty. The gauge is showing you that something bad is about to happen (running out of petrol isn't good). Naturally you don't just do nothing. On the contrary, you stop at the next service station to buy petrol. Once you have filled the tank, you don't continuously check the petrol gauge to see how much you have left. You don't let it monopolise your thoughts. If you did, your driving would become erratic and possibly dangerous. The same goes for negative thoughts, uncertainties, and fears; if you are continually assailed by threats to the point where they monopolise your life, you will find it very difficult to be creative. This is a question of emotion and perception.

People who score high on a standard happiness test solve twenty-five percent more creative challenges than those who feel uneasy or irritable. Positive mental states enable you to relax more, which means you focus less on the world's problems and you are better at associating disparate concepts. However, a degree of melancholy sharpens your attention, allowing you to be more concentrated and tenacious in your chosen activity. Various studies show that famous authors are eight times more likely than the general population to suffer from some form of severe depression. It isn't that successful artists are crazier, they are just unhappier.

Perceptions and emotions

'Making the simple complicated, that's commonplace,
making the complicated simple, awesomely simple,
that's creativity.'

Charles Mingus

A while ago I read a story about a pygmy who left his dense
jungle habitat for the first time and was driven by car out onto
the African plains. Halfway through the journey, the pygmy
observes an insect ahead of him. As the car moves along, he
becomes increasingly surprised at how the insect is growing
bigger and bigger. Utterly bewildered, he asks the driver
what magical insect this is. The driver tells him that what they
are approaching isn't an insect, it's a buffalo. The dominant
perceptions in the pygmy's brain (insects in the jungle) made
him assume that the buffalo was an insect.

All our dominant perceptions influence our behaviour and
the ideas we have. Our neural networks are responsible for how
we see and understand the world. They are like a system of
meanings, which, through perception, helps us to make sense
of what we see, while at the same time providing us with rules
that shape our **interactions** with the world. They exist through
a combination of inherited genetic elements and experience.

Physical environment also has a big impact on our neural
networks. Because of the denseness of the jungle where our
pygmy friend lives, he is accustomed to seeing only a few yards
in front of him. His ability to perceive has been shaped in such
a way that he can understand the situation in his natural habitat,

not out on the plains, not when he sees buffalos. The cultures we grow up in are exposed to and affected by the paradigms we construct. Any type of group, profession or discipline has its own assumptions about reality; what is possible, what is acceptable, worthwhile, and so on. We assimilate those paradigms and pass them on through culture and tradition to subsequent generations: birthdays, funerals, weddings, watching football on Sundays. Friends, relatives, work colleagues, fellow students at school and university, teachers, also influence our perceptions. It is easier for humans to communicate amongst themselves when they share similar outlooks on the world, because they share the same meanings, the same understanding.

If we cling to our paradigms, we become blind to other people's ideas about the world, other possibilities, perceptions, solutions or ideas. This poses a problem for our creativity. Our assumptions prevent us from moving forward, from thinking differently and being more creative. Simply being aware of this is a positive first step towards changing our assumptions and thinking outside the box.

Preconceptions

We are full of preconceptions and they can block our creativity.

Exercise: give five different names to things that already have names.

For example, you could call music 'sounds that fly' or clouds 'white smoke that drifts up high'.

Exercise: Pretend you are a camera.

Walk around the room, or wherever you are, with your eyes closed – making sure you don't bump into things, of course.

Stop whenever you like.

Open and close your eyes very fast as if you were taking snapshots.

Look at what's in front of you without any preconceptions.

Retain the images you see in rapid sequence. This will help you see what is actually there, not filtered through your expectations.

When confronting a new problem, it is vital for the creative process that we reduce the number of preconceptions we have.

One of the reasons why our assumptions exert such a strong influence over us is because of our emotions. As we saw at the beginning of this section, our emotional responses to circumstances or situations can be triggered very quickly by specific perceptions or interpretations. For example, when we are unable to concentrate on writing a report at work, we become discouraged and feel that it's hopeless, that we'll never get it done. If in the street a stranger asks us something in a foreign language, we will get frustrated because we don't understand what they are saying. If we are approached by someone who dresses very differently from us, we will feel afraid. We perceive as dangerous situations that are in fact harmless and we start to fantasise and over-interpret our experiences, often completely unaware of how appropriate our responses are to the actual situation. Our past experiences inform our present emotions: an emotional response can provoke an intellectual response, which in turn perpetuates our emotions. A simple gesture can be interpreted as an affront.

However, these emotional responses, through our unconsciousness, also help us to maintain a degree of equilibrium; they supply us with the energy to run away or fight in the event of a real attack, although in today's world a lot of that energy is squandered in situations that don't represent a real threat. When our emotional responses are triggered unconsciously in any kind of situation, it distorts our perceptions. To avoid this, *we must start to develop a more conscious relationship with our emotions*, to try to get to know them better, to understand what they are telling us. *Let's remember that the most creative people on the planet are those who profess to know themselves extremely well.*

We have a tendency to interpret and overreact to things. So, why not stop, take a deep breath and try to put the real situation into perspective?

Assumptions can be disastrous for the creative process because they limit how we look at our challenge

Ask yourself: are you making assumptions about your challenge, which are artificially limiting your options? Possibly as a result of past experiences, something your father said to you, or something you heard at a meeting, which you are trying to avoid.

Exaggerated responses also have a biological explanation. The more often an experience is repeated the stronger our neural connections become. The more often we are exposed to a thing or person, the stronger the associations it has in our brain. Donald Hebb explains that the more frequently a group of neurons is activated simultaneously, the more efficient the signalling between those neurons becomes. When you oil a door hinge, the door will open more easily. Each new experience tends simply to reinforce what we already know. That's why we have evolved to enjoy the things that are familiar to us, the sense of security that offers and, on the other hand, to fear the unknown. The tensions that can arise between people with different viewpoints or ways of looking at life have a neurological basis. During our evolutionary struggle, it seems we humans decided that our best hope of survival was to establish continuity between ourselves and our surroundings. When that balance is disturbed by different customs, beliefs, or traditions, or a change in our physical environment, we feel uncomfortable and threatened. That is when prejudices appear.

All of the above reasons explain why we find it so difficult to deviate from the norm, to be creative: because a lot of our biology is telling us to stick with what we know. If we are accustomed to particular processes, ways of dealing with problems or guaranteed methods of success, we will feel **uncomfortable** when new ones appear. The same applies to our ideas and behaviour. When the outside world no longer coincides with our inner world, a biological response is triggered inside us that requires us either to change our environment or change our internal structures – i.e. the way things are, or the way we think they should be. This predisposition to stick with what we know is what makes it so difficult to think differently. Being creative is a huge challenge. But it is possible.

> *Striving to transform yourself into someone brilliant and productive without changing your basic habits and the structure of your life is a waste of effort.*

From anxiety to fear

Having butterflies in your stomach before a public presentation is nothing out of the ordinary. However, everyday anxieties can sometimes become intense, paralysing fears we call phobias. If these phobias are left untreated, they can prevent people from enjoying the things that make up our daily life. To an outside observer, the cause of such fears may not appear to constitute a real threat, but to the phobic person their fear is as palpable as if there were an actual threat.

Such phobias (fear of heights, open spaces, spiders, public speaking) generally begin in childhood or adolescence, although many sufferers can't recall a specific trigger. They also appear to have a genetic component. At present, cognitive behavioural therapy (CBT) seems to be one of the most successful methods of reducing or eliminating phobias. CBT practitioners occasionally use drugs that block fear, so that patients can be helped slowly to face their fears and then gradually overcome them without the need for medication. It seems that being exposed in a repeated and controlled way to the source of our fears, without any negative consequences, diminishes their hold over us. Taking small steps is crucial. A therapist treating patients with vertigo, for example, might start by showing them a photograph taken from the roof of a low building. Then, as they begin to relax, the therapist intensifies the exposure in a controlled environment. Patients might be asked to imagine a balcony, for example, and then be taken to an elevated but safe place and made to stand there. Eventually, their anxiety subsides and the phobia gradually disappears.

Anger

Anger management is designed to control the physical responses that result from anger. It doesn't remove the causes of our anger or our capacity to experience that emotion. Nor is it about telling people to 'calm down': it has been shown that suppressing anger is bad for our relationships and for our mental health, like plugging an erupting volcano. Managing anger reduces the impact which the emotion has on our body and enables us to control our experience. There are books about anger-management. These are some of the basic steps:

▲ Breathe deeply from your belly; while you are breathing, repeat a word or sentence that calms you such as 'relax'; visualise a peaceful scene such as a beach, rolling hills or a mountain range; perform some slow, calming exercises.
▲ Use your imagination; visualise a relaxing experience, such a lying in a hammock.

▲ Remind yourself that acting on the cause of your anger and irritation won't solve your problems. Only calculated, purposeful action will do that. Learn to communicate better with those around you. Listen. Speak calmly. Reassess your situation using positive language. Instead of cursing and describing your life as hopeless, look at your situation in a rational way. Tell yourself that things aren't so bad, and that you will pull through. The prefrontal cortex is speaking to the limbic system. Reformulating, as we saw at the beginning of this section.

Great, I'm irritated

In the early 1900s, people found having to slice their own bread irritating. Otto Frederick Rohwedder spent seventeen years of his life and invested all his money in inventing a mechanical bread-slicing machine. Otto ended up bankrupt because no one in the industry wanted to buy his machine. However, thirty years later a company called Continental adopted the machine and called it Wonder Bread. Within a year, eighty percent of all the bread sold was sliced. Otto claimed that being obliged to slice his own bread was what inspired him to create something new, not the prospect of making money.

Ideas often grow from things that irritate us. Write down a list of things that irritate you. Select a few challenges that might lead to something interesting.

Creative fears

Humans have evolved certain characteristics that made it possible for our ancestors to form groups, develop new technologies and overcome predators. Fear is undeniably a valuable tool in some situations. If you are standing on the roof of a twenty-storey building staring into the abyss, a modicum of fear will make you take a few steps back. As I wait to cross a busy road with my daughter, I will clasp her hand more tightly. These sorts of fear are essential to our survival. However, there are others, which, if we let them dictate our behaviour, will prevent us from performing actions or tasks to our full potential. Creativity often suffers because of the fear of what 'might be'. 'Let's go for the safe option,' we tell ourselves. The possible consequences of making what we feel might be a fatal blunder are exaggerated, and in order to avoid them we end up doing a mediocre job. Occasionally these fears come from outside: for example, our boss tells us: 'if you mess this up, you're fired'. But most of the time our own fears of being noticed, in a good or a bad way, or of being given the cold shoulder by friends or colleagues, plays an important role.

> Comfort is the enemy of greatness. When you choose comfort, you are choosing mediocrity.

When we think about creative fears, we usually mean fear of failure. We don't want to mess up, so we take fewer risks. We have been doing the same job for a long time, and have learned to do it reasonably well, without taking any risks. *All creative work is the result of taking risks.* We have to look beyond our current situation and risk possible failure. As the author Peter Block says, 'Live at the margins, not at the centre.' Our fears aren't unfounded. If we attempt to go beyond the known, some people are bound to think our ideas are mistaken. We feel threatened by this, and as we saw earlier, our primitive brain continually steers us away from threat and towards the security of the familiar, the known. After all, those animals that stray from the group are the first to be eaten by predators. You must *learn to identify and to avoid the impulses of your survival instinct.* This requires you to be aware and highly attentive to what you are doing, and to learn to take calculated risks. You can start to do that in areas where there is no outside pressure to succeed so it won't matter if you make a mistake.

Ask yourself: in what way is fear of failure restricting your creativity? When do you refuse to take risks in your life and in your work? What are the perceived consequences that prevent you from acting? Do you think they are real or imagined?

Another, more subconscious, fear which many people have when faced with a creative challenge is the fear of success: a sort of paranoid voice telling us we won't be able to go on getting such good results, or we won't be up to the job when it comes to implementing our creative idea. This makes us pull back from committing ourselves fully to our creative challenge, because we don't want to grapple with the consequences of success. Some people spend their whole lives struggling with fears like these, convinced that everything they do is out of their league. They feel they are in the bottom division when they could be playing for the top division. These subtle but destructive impulses stunt our growth. Although when we grow we can sometimes feel awkward, without awkwardness our capacity to develop doesn't remain the same, it diminishes. If we don't grow, we die. That is why fear of success can often be more destructive than fear of failure, because it hides behind a mask of common sense; it appears companionable, or as if we are adopting a grown-up attitude, but all it does is cause us to miss opportunities.

> Ask yourself: Are you becoming less creative because you are afraid you won't be able to keep it up in the long term? Have you ever blocked a creative idea because you fear the consequences? Do you feel indifferent to success in life or your work?

Stress

One of the great difficulties with stress is to know when someone is experiencing it. Some people find parachuting fun, while others turn pale just thinking about it. Measuring cortisol levels can be a useful tool, but there is no single group of physiological responses that can tell a scientist when someone is experiencing stress. Many of the mechanisms that cause stress when we see a predator are also present in the brain when we have sex or eat an ice cream. Stress and pleasure are both characterised by a state of heightened physiological excitement. However, according to the expert David Diamond, we know we are stressed when the following three situations occur simultaneously:

1) *A state of physiological excitement must be observable to a third party.* When that ass Ortega got sent off during the World Cup match against Holland in '98, I (the third party) could see Argentinian fans shouting and crying, perspiring freely as they clutched their heads in despair.

2) *The stimulus causing the stress must be 'aversive'.* Ask yourself whether, if you could, you would lower the intensity of what you are experiencing. If the answer is yes, then the stimulus is 'aversive'. The fans would clearly have preferred Ortega to remain on the field and so his being sent off was an aversive stimulus.

3) *You feel you have no control over the stimulus causing your physiological excitement.* The less control you have, the more severe the perceived stress. The fans had zero control over Ortega's behaviour or the referee's decision to give him a red card.

These three components occurring simultaneously in our bodies generate what we call stress.

When your sensory system detects danger, besides increasing your heart rate and blood pressure, your hypothalamus secretes massive amounts of adrenalin, which gives us the extra energy to fight or flee. A less well-known hormone – the above-mentioned cortisol – is also secreted, but by the adrenal glands themselves. Without this swift, flexible and highly regulated system of response to danger, we would perish. However, this system was designed to deal with immediate not long-term situations, in particular to enable our muscles to move as fast as possible when confronted with danger. The stressful situations we encounter today have nothing in common with the instant it takes for a lion to charge. They can last hours, days or years: problems at work, money troubles, family feuds, etc. Small amounts of cortisol start to build up in our bloodstream, and when this goes on for months rather than days, they become toxic. This is how imbalances occur in our *delicate* system that can affect our performance at work. It is why people suffering from chronic stress are up to three times more likely to fall ill, and have an increased risk of heart attack. Our system wasn't built to deal efficiently with modern human life.

Another adverse effect of prolonged stress is that it drives people into depression. One study suggests that as many as eight hundred thousand people take their own lives every year due to severe depression. Eighty percent of all spending on healthcare in the developed world is used to treat stress-related illness. Seventy-seven percent of people working in companies say they have experienced states of 'exhaustion' and 'burn-out', which means raised levels of cortisol, lots of missed meetings, and doctor's appointments.

So, with prolonged levels of extreme stress comes a prolonged exposure to cortisol. Various studies show that this can damage the brain and the hippocampus, impeding our ability to memorise and learn new things, which is essential to our creativity. Individuals suffering from stress perform poorly at maths, can't process language properly and have worse memories (both short and long term). They also have difficulty adapting old information to new situations, suffer from poor concentration and show reduced performance. It appears that stress arises in the workplace or at home when there is a combination of high expectation and an inability to perform. Stress at home affects performance at work and vice versa, creating an increasingly destructive vicious circle.

The most effective way to manage stress is maintaining as much control as possible over our life. In order to diminish the impact of stress, we need to lower our cortisol levels. A few tried and tested ways of doing this are:

- ▲ Slow your thoughts through meditation.
- ▲ Practise breathing exercises and yoga.
- ▲ Maintain links with family and close friends.
- ▲ Laugh; laughing increases the amount of oxygen we inhale and releases endorphins.
- ▲ Make sure you are well rested; being very tired can increase stress levels, but sleeping lowers them.
- ▲ Take exercise, physical activity reduces stress.

Run, run, run

'For me, running is both exercise and a metaphor. Running day after day, piling up the races, bit by bit I raise the bar, and by clearing each level I elevate myself. At least that's why I've put in the effort day after day: to raise my own level.'

Haruki Murakami

We have already established that a healthy mental state is associated with the increased appearance of insights. It is also said: *a sound mind in a sound body.*

Although there is still much controversy on the subject of human evolutionary history, one idea which no anthropologist or palaeontologist will contest is that our ancestors were in constant movement. Rather than move up and down between the ground and the trees, depending on the climate at the time, they moved in two directions, criss-crossing the planet in search of a more favourable environment in which to live. That requires an awful lot of walking; it is thought between six and twelve miles a day for men and three to six miles for women. Our modern brain evolved while we were extremely physically active: we were like a species of marathon runner.

That was a hundred thousand years ago when we humans started to leave Africa, and we reached Europe forty thousand years ago. We crossed rivers, deserts, jungles, mountains and seas. Our ancestors were constantly seeking out new food sources, identifying predators and physical dangers. This data suggests that we evolved with a very robust physique; movement was a constant feature of human existence. It is quite possible that our entire cognitive ability, including our creativity, developed precisely during the time when we sustained this intense level of physical activity.

In today's world, one of the great predictors of a healthy old age is the presence or absence of a sedentary lifestyle. All evidence suggests that exercise improves the cardiovascular system and reduces the risk of illnesses such as heart attack or stroke. In addition, our physical health greatly affects how we score on every type of cognitive test (long- and short-term memory, analytical and critical reasoning, attention, problem-solving ability, ability to think quickly or in an abstract way, psychomotor speed, etc.) Someone who has always practised physical exercise invariably performs better in cognitive tests than someone who has led a sedentary life. This shows a link between physical and mental fitness, though not a causal one. However, when sedentary people improve their physical state, their cognitive state also improves.

Many such experiments have been carried out, proving beyond doubt that being in good shape physically stimulates our cognitive ability. For example, the risk of dementia is halved in people who have carried out a physical activity all their lives. The effect of exercise on mood is so important that many psychiatrists have started prescribing it. Exercise is also beneficial in treating depression and anxiety both in the short and long term, and works equally for men and women. The longer the exercise session, the better the results.

Physical exercise

As we saw earlier, although the brain represents between two and five percent of our body weight, it can consume as much as twenty-five percent of our energy requirements. When the brain is working at full throttle, it uses up more energy per gram of tissue than the quadriceps during a workout. Our brain is unable to activate more than two percent of our neurons at any one time. We can survive without food for about a month, and without water for about a week. However, our brain is so active that it can't be deprived of oxygen for more than five minutes; if that happens we either die or suffer irreversible brain damage. When the blood can't transport enough oxygen to the brain, toxins start to accumulate. We now know that even in a completely healthy brain it is always possible to improve blood flow, i.e. the transportation of oxygen. And this is achieved through exercise. Exercise doesn't necessarily deliver more oxygen and calories to the brain, but it provides better access to them. Exercise increases the number and extension of all arteries and blood vessels, including those in the brain. This happens because exercising stimulates the production of a much-studied molecule called nitric oxide responsible for regulating blood flow. As blood flow improves, the body produces an increased number of blood vessels that penetrate more deeply into its tissues: in other words it provides more access to energy and oxygen, it improves energy distribution and it rids the circulation of toxins.

Physical activity is often referred to as *brain food*. Studies using brain-imaging techniques show how exercise literally increases the blood flow to different areas of the brain. Another effect of exercise on the brain that has also been studied is the stimulation of the production of a powerful family of proteins called neurotrophins, which keep neurons young, healthy and able to connect with one another. Neurotrophins also stimulate neurogenesis, the formation of new neurons in the brain.

So, when talking about creativity and keeping the brain healthy and ready to fulfil the demands of creative thinking, I wouldn't be surprised if in the near future companies, businesses and organisations were to install, for example, treadmills for walking or running during meetings, as well as providing morning and afternoon breaks for employees to take exercise. Schools could get rid of the traditional desks and let pupils walk around during class, while they attend a maths lesson. Let's remember that our ancestors who lived in Africa didn't sit in classrooms, they were literally constantly on the move; if one of them had been forced to sit in the same place for eight hours, or even one, they would have ended up becoming lunch or dinner for another predator. We haven't had millions of years in which to adapt to our new, sedentary lifestyle. The way we live is incompatible with the optimum needs of the brain that allow it to function as efficiently as possible. Close this book and take a long walk around the block.

Love

'It's not about money or talent. It's about creativity and love.'

Amy Butler

'I no longer love her, that's certain, but maybe I love her, love is so short and forgetting so long.'

Pablo Neruda

It is quite logical to assume that love is a universal feeling. And the fact that it is the same or very similar the world over suggests that certain chemical components and brain networks must play a part in this beautiful, and occasionally troublesome, emotion.

It goes without saying that for science it is the brain not the heart that is responsible for what happens to us during those first few months of passion and beyond. Rather unromantically, we know that when our brain is in love it is not dissimilar to when we are mentally ill or under the influence of cocaine. An even less romantic possibility is that when we feel attracted to someone it is because unconsciously we like his or her genes. Sight alone isn't responsible for whether we like someone; smell also plays an important role, and, at the risk of removing all romanticism from the equation, we are attracted to the 'smell' that most resembles that of our parents. Thus the Cupid's arrow within us contains a veritable chemical arsenal. Where love is concerned, we are at the mercy of our biochemistry; the activation of certain regions of the brain stimulates the heart and gives us butterflies in our stomach. Helen Fisher, probably the foremost expert on falling in love, describes three stages where our chemistry plays an important role: desire or lust, falling in love or attraction, and affection or attachment. The first stage, lust, is guided by the sex hormones testosterone and oestrogen; at this point we haven't yet found our supposed other half, but we are highly aroused. In the attraction stage we are obsessed, and all we think about is the one we love; this stage is associated with a drop in serotonin levels and an increase in dopamine and norepinephrine levels.

In experiments carried out at the Albert Einstein College of Medicine, researchers wondered what would happen if people in love were hooked up to an MRI scanner and shown a photograph of their beloved. To establish a comparison, the enamoured subjects were then shown images of people they knew at school or university. In between the two photographs, they were shown a number (8,421) and asked to count backwards seven digits. The distraction task was to prevent any feelings provoked by the photograph of their beloved from contaminating their response to the 'neutral' photograph. Although several regions of the brain were activated when the subjects were shown the photograph of their beloved, two in particular appeared to receive the most oxygen and glucose – i.e. they were most active: one is the area known as the 'caudate nucleus', which is part of our most primitive, reptilian brain, and controls movement and the reward system network, and which is activated when we experience feelings of pleasure and the desire for gratification. The more passionate the subjects (measured on a scale of 'passionate love' based on the declarations of the participants), the more activity occurred in that region. Another part of the brain that showed increased activity was the part that lights up when we eat chocolate, and for those who think that love is a drug, there is your confirmation. And finally, the ventral tegmental area or VTA, part of the reward system network and a major secretor of dopamine and norepinephrine revealed itself in all its splendour. When dopamine is distributed to other areas of the brain, it creates enormous focus, a sensation of heightened energy, a strong impulse to obtain a reward, as well as joy and euphoria (which can sometimes become mania) – in short all the feelings and behaviour patterns we know so well, and which are a central part of falling in love. Flooded with dopamine, and forcefully, single-mindedly focused on obtaining our goal, the entire apparatus of our brain working at full throttle, it is no small wonder we can't sleep, that we send thousands of emails and text messages every day, change jobs and lifestyles, smother each other with hugs and kisses, and sometimes even die for love. In other words, this stage isn't simply a strong emotion we experience as love, but rather a combination of that emotion and the important role played by the reward system. The motivation to obtain what we want.

In a similar experiment, at Stanford University, a study was also made of the effects of being in love and its analgesic power. The area of the brain under scrutiny is known as the *nucleus accumbens*, and is central to the rewards associated with addiction to opioids, cocaine and other drugs. In subjects who are in love it was found to be in full synaptic action, suggesting that drugs aren't the only things that prevent pain: when we are in love things hurt less.

The final stage kicks in if the relationship is meant to last. Sadly, the enamoured phase can't last for ever; if it did we would be incapable of doing anything else with our lives. In this last stage, the nervous system secretes the hormone oxytocin, associated with childbirth and breastfeeding in women. This hormone helps to establish a bond between mother and baby. It is also secreted in both men and women during orgasm, and the theory is that the more sex a couple has, the stronger the bond between them, though I am sure not everyone will agree with that. The other hormone secreted in this final stage is vasopressin, an important molecule in long-term relationships.

What an elegant idea, that passion should emanate from the *caudate nucleus*, the motor of our brain that has been evolutionarily preserved, that it should sprinkle us with dopamine, that most natural of all stimulants. Passion becomes naturally entwined with two of our other basic instincts: reproduction and the drive to build deep and lasting relationships. Increasing our understanding of how we fall in love, or why when our love is unrequited we become 'heartbroken', might help us to develop new therapies to treat the depression and stress caused by lovesickness.

Emily Dickinson said: 'the brain is wider than the sky', and how wonderful that this is true. Numerous studies have shown that we are more creative when we are in love. Love, it seems, changes our thoughts, triggering a generalised process in our brain, which stimulates the connections between disparate non-specialised areas (what happens just before an insight) and interferes with analytical thought. It also prompts thoughts with a view to the long term, helping us to see the wood for the trees – meaning before detail. And that in turn encourages the appearance of new ideas.

LEARNING

I learn, therefore I am

> 'I never let my school interfere with my education.'
>
> Mark Twain

> 'You can't teach a man anything; you can only help
> him to find the answer within himself.'
>
> Galileo Galilei

For decades, scientists were convinced that we were born a blank canvas, an empty space, a hard drive without any data. They thought that babies learned everything through their interaction with the environment, above all with adults. We now know this isn't true. When we come into the world our hard drive, our brain, is preloaded with data-processing software.

In a legendary experiment in 1979, Professor Andrew Meltzoff changed the world of child psychology when he poked his tongue out at a baby and waited to see whether the baby would return the gesture. Amazingly, the baby, which was only forty-two minutes old, did precisely that. Obviously it had never seen a tongue before, its own or anyone else's. And yet the baby knew it had a tongue, it knew that Meltzoff had a tongue, and somehow it instinctively mirrored his gesture. We could go even further and conclude that the baby knew that by stimulating a series of nerves in a particular sequence, it too could poke out its tongue; in short, the opposite of a blank canvas. For this and many other reasons, as we mentioned earlier, children and babies make the best guinea pigs when attempting to understand how humans acquire information.

If we study the mind of a child, we see that we are all born with a deep desire to understand the world around us, and an insatiable curiosity that compels us to explore everything we encounter. This curiosity is so powerful that some scientists compare it to our impulses when confronted by hunger, thirst or sex. In another famous set of experiments, a group of babies was given a rake, and a toy which was placed far away from them. The babies soon learned to use the rake to get the toy. Parents often observe this kind of behaviour at home. However, after a few successful attempts the babies lost interest, but not in the game per se. They moved the toy to different places and then used the rake to get it again. Sometimes they even put the toy in unreachable places to see what the rake could do. They were experimenting with the relationship between objects, specifically with how one object could influence another; in other words the babies appeared interested in the physical properties of objects. Infants under twelve months old will investigate all kinds of objects with their sensory arsenal; kicking, shaking, licking, placing them in other people's mouth, etc. They avidly seek information about an object's properties, which, to the chagrin of adults, often means those objects turn up broken.

Another interesting idea, much researched in infants, and which has implications for the evolution and survival of the human race, is known as object permanence. For a child under eighteen months old, an object hidden beneath a handkerchief has 'disappeared'. Afterwards, the baby will begin to experiment with covering and uncovering objects with the handkerchief until it realises, with great joy and excitement, that not seeing something doesn't mean it has disappeared. Object permanence was essential when we were still living on the African plain. A crouching leopard hidden in the tall grass hasn't disappeared. Those who failed to acquire that knowledge undoubtedly ended up on the leopard's menu.

Around that age we also learn that people have preferences and desires that are different from ours. Before the age of two, babies do a lot of things their parents would prefer them not to do. However, after the age of two they do those things *because* their parents don't want them to. They seem to turn into little tyrants or rebels, and many parents feel their children are defying them. In fact, it is the natural expression of a sophisticated process of investigation that is just beginning. Infants push the limits of other people's preferences then let go to see how they react. They repeat the experiment again and again to see how stable their discoveries are, and to make sure the limits are still there. Gradually they learn what other people's desires are and how they differ from their own. Babies may not understand much about the world but they certainly know how to extract information from it.

When it comes to how we learn, Eric Kandel, whose theory of intelligent memory we looked at earlier, is the leading expert. Kandel also showed how a simple piece of new information changes the structure of the neurons that take part in the process. As we learn, our brain changes the organisation and reorganisation of its structure. And, since we are constantly learning, it stands to reason that the brain is constantly rewiring itself. In other words, the brain is like a muscle; the more active it is, the bigger and more complex it becomes. What we do in our lives literally changes our brain. Even the brains of identical twins aren't the same. At birth our brain is only partially assembled. The main period of construction ends when we are around twenty, but it continues to hone itself until our mid-forties. The number of neural connections in a newborn is the same as in an adult, but at three years old that number doubles or triples in some areas of the brain, returning to the original number at around aged eight. This happens again during puberty; only the regions and areas of the brain that develop are different. However, some studies show that these regions develop at different rates in different children. Just as when you look at a class of teenagers you will see that some are more physically developed than others, the same applies to the brain.

Another expert on learning and memory is Richard Mayer, who spent decades studying the effects of multimedia learning. His five main conclusions, obtained from empirical data about how humans learn best, are listed below (some of them coincide with what we have learned about our vision):

1) We learn better with words and images than with words alone.
2) We learn better when the words and images are presented simultaneously as opposed to consecutively.
3) We learn better when the words and images are close together.
4) We learn better when any irrelevant material is removed from the presentation.
5) We learn more with animated images and narration than with animated images and text on a screen.

Mirror, mirror on the wall, who is the fairest of us all?

In 1991, three researchers from the University of Parma, founded in the eleventh century, led by Dr Giacomo Rizzolatti, were looking at how a macaque's brain lit up when it reached for different objects. One day, a researcher took a raisin off a plate and noticed how the primate's brain, which was hooked up to electrodes, became activated. The animal's brain pattern suggested that it was picking up the raisin itself instead of seeing the Italian scientist pick it up. After repeating the experiment and making further discoveries, the researchers inferred the existence of what we know today as mirror neurons, whose activity reflects what is going on around us.

Mirror neurons were quickly discovered in humans, and have become a very fashionable area of study in neuroscience today. Thanks to these neurons, babies are able to poke out their tongue in imitation of an adult, minutes after being born, as Andrew Meltzoff observed in 1979. The theory determines that when you see someone carrying out an action like kicking a ball, skipping, washing up, grilling a steak, those neurons instantly simulate the action in your own brain. According to Dr Vilayanur Ramachandran, mirror neurons evolved to help us recognise valuable information more quickly.

Imagine a hundred thousand years ago, when human culture was in its infancy (using tools, lighting fires, building shelters, using language, etc.), rather than learn and relearn 'how to make fire', as we watch someone else do it, mirror neurons make us 'feel' as if we were lighting the fire ourselves; they unconsciously imitate the actions of others.

This is known as the ability to 'live' the experience of another, and is fundamental for species that learn quickly the different abilities of members of its own group. It is as if besides the vertical teaching of parents and the horizontal teaching of other members of the community, we also learn exponentially thanks to those neurons. Cookery programmes on TV are a perfect example of this: we learn much more quickly if we see someone preparing a dish than if we read a recipe. When a well-known car manufacturer projected onto giant screens images of a sleek sports car driving through different countries and landscapes with the aim of luring people into its showroom, it discovered that passers-by stopped for an average of eighty-seven seconds. But when they changed the film and showed the driver steering the car, opening the roof, turning on the radio, etc., people stopped for an average of one hundred and forty-three seconds, and sales of the car increased among people of both sexes and over all age ranges. Our mirror neurons 'live' the experience of driving that sports car through exotic landscapes, and we enjoy it.

Challenge yourself

Create or generate a minimum number of ideas per day – say, five or ten. You will see that your first ideas of the week will be difficult to generate. But those ideas will bring other ideas, which will connect with still other ideas, until gradually the exercise becomes easier.

Setting yourself a minimum number of ideas forces you actively to generate those ideas, and other alternative ones, instead of waiting for them to arise.

For example, Thomas Edison set himself the goal of inventing something small every ten days and something significant every six months.

There have been many recent studies of mirror neurons involving touch, movement, intentions and emotions. For example, when you read the word 'itch' in the right context you will start to itch, when you read the words 'I kick the ball' the motor intention areas in your brain are activated, and when you hear the word 'jump', movement preparation areas are activated.

Many athletes use a visualisation technique before an important contest. They imagine they are completing an action before they actually carry it out, and they maintain that this improves their performance. We now know that watching someone carry out a task or activity can also improve our performance, and that this is due to the actions of mirror neurons. It is normal for musicians to learn more quickly from watching their teacher play. Note, however, that this is only true when people practise the same activity: if I watch Nadal play tennis all day, my mirror neurons will play tennis too, but unless I am a tennis player it won't improve my performance.

Mirror neurons in everyday life: when parents watch their children being vaccinated they also experience pain; when you see a friend having a stressful conversation your blood pressure goes up; when you see a cyclist go down a hill very fast it makes your pulse race, you secrete more endorphins and become more alert; you see a colleague closing a deal and it gives you a feeling of pleasure and success. Sound effects on the radio (which is only heard not seen) that 'draw' the listeners in to the activity being described, make those neurons fire, increase our interest and possibly even motivate us to follow a programme.

We could sum up by saying that our survival depended, and still depends, a lot on our ability to understand the actions, intentions and emotions of others. We now know that our ability to simulate them automatically without having to think, rationalise and analyse is due to a variety of mirror neurons.

Today there is a lot of evidence to suggest that some areas of the adult brain are as malleable as that of a baby. Our brains can make new connections, strengthen those that already exist and even generate new neurons. Because of this we are able to continue learning throughout our lives. This is a fairly recent discovery, and up until about a decade ago, it was believed that we were born with a finite number of neurons. The news isn't all good, because we also lose synaptic connections as we age, some estimate around thirty thousand every day. However, the adult brain is able *to create* neurons in the regions associated with learning, and they show the same plasticity as those found in babies. Fortunately, the brain maintains the ability to adapt its structure and function in response to our experience throughout its lifetime.

As for learning and creativity, we should learn more from our children; they understand very well that discovery brings enjoyment, satisfaction and happiness. Like an addictive drug, exploring through curiosity creates a further need to discover in order to experience more enjoyment. It is a clear example of the reward system at work, and if we let it blossom in our children, they will carry it through school.

> To create is to explore possibilities!

As we grow up, we discover that learning not only makes us happy but that through it we can also become experts. Specialising in an area gives us the confidence to take certain intellectual risks. If our children don't end up in casualty, they may end up in Sweden receiving a Nobel Prize. Sadly, as we mentioned in chapter one, we adults put this natural cycle of learning-happiness to sleep. When children enter primary school, they learn that education means passing exams. They learn to acquire information not because it is interesting but as a means to an end. Interest takes a back seat, and the most common question becomes, what do I have to do to pass the exam?

And yet, we only have to look at history to see that many people aren't taken in by society's message and their innate curiosity and desire to explore makes them flourish. To give a very recent, modern-day example, the company Google allows employees twenty percent leisure time to explore and let their minds wander freely. The results are remarkable, and fifty percent of Google's products (including Gmail and Google News) are generated during that leisure time. This is a good moment to ask ourselves how we could adapt that freedom to explore for use in our offices and classrooms. This leisure time, what Google call 'Innovation Time off' was started long before by 3M (The Minnesota Mining and Manufacturing Company), a company that has been inventing new products for the last seventy-five years, and was recently ranked as the third most innovative company after Apple and Google. Among its most well-known products are Post-it notes and transparent sticky tape.

The success of 3M is largely due to its policy of 'flexible attention'; instead of asking employees to focus their attention continuously for eight hours every day, they encourage them to carry out activities which at first sight might not seem very productive, like strolling in the park, relaxing in an armchair and gazing out of the window, daydreaming. We have already seen that insights arise more frequently during moments of relaxation and enjoyment. If you are stuck on a problem, go out for a walk. The only obligation employees at 3M have is to share their ideas with their colleagues. Input from other people with different perspectives and experiences improves ideas and will often lead to them being implemented.

As we saw earlier, the brain has developed in subtle ways to be able to respond to threats, attacks, aggression, to detect truth and falsehoods, to avoid disappointment. Our brains are more often than not set on 'emergency mode', due to the overstimulation of our modern lifestyle.

Why, if we are such intelligent creatures, have we evolved in such a way as to create such a hostile, stressful environment? Perhaps because we are ambitious and creative at the same time. We never conform to what is, and are constantly striving to find better solutions. We pay a high price for our creations, but we also receive good rewards: we have eradicated diseases, created great works of art, decoded the human genome, and we can communicate with other people anywhere in the world. All thanks to the fact that we use our cerebral database and can improvise on it; we are logical and creative at the same time. But whereas logic is being taught and learned continuously at school, at home, at work, and in society, the same can't be said of creativity. Let's use the remainder of this book to learn how to be even more creative.

Provocation

Widely used to break established patterns and to discover unorthodox ideas.

Write a provocative statement (however silly or absurd): 'swimming pools don't need water'.

Continued

Explore the pros and cons of what you have written and the ideas the statement gives you: building cushioned swimming pools, filling them with foam balls, organising art exhibitions in empty swimming pools.

Magazines

Buy four or five magazines you would never usually buy (on travel, cigars, horticulture, interior design, etc.)

Pick a page at random.

Turn to that page in all of your magazines and look at what you see (a photograph, drawing, article, an advert, etc.)

Concentrate on that and try to relate it to your creative challenge.

The dancer

Find a video of a dancer performing on an art channel or on YouTube (it might be classical, jazz, contemporary or the lambada).

Concentrate very hard on the dance, and keep watching for a moment or two without stopping.

Write down a noun, a verb, an adjective and an adverb to describe your experience while you were watching, what the dance conjured up for you.

Relate those four words to your creative challenge.

I forgot that I forgot you

During the first moments when we learn something, we are able to remember it. The brain has different types of memory, many of which function semi-automatically. Very little is yet known about the coordination of those different types of memory, but we do know that memory isn't considered a unique phenomenon. We could imagine it as an intruder, an invader that allows our past experiences to impinge continuously on our present.

As we grow, our brain is formed by our experience thanks to memory. For such fragile creatures as human beings, in the middle of the African plain, having no memory, being unable to remember not to repeat the same mistakes and fall in the same traps would doubtless have signified the end of the species. All human cognitive ability, like reading, writing or speaking, exists because of memory. Memory, then, is not only responsible for our survival, it also makes us human.

Amazingly, within thirty days, we have usually forgotten around ninety percent of what we learn in a class or a talk, and we forget most of that within the first few hours. It is now a well-established fact that we can increase how long we remember things simply by repeating the information at specific intervals. The length of time between repetitions is crucial to transforming short-term memories into long-term ones. Remembering our mobile phone number isn't difficult, and yet often when we scan our memory for that number we need to visualise the last time we saw it or remember the last time we wrote it down. Remembering how to ride a bicycle is completely different; we have no list or detailed procedure about where to place our feet or how to sit, hold the handlebars, etc.; and yet, we remember how to ride a bicycle in the same way as we remember an eleven digit mobile number. So, we have a memory that involves conscious attention – declarative memory (phone number), and another that doesn't – nondeclarative memory (motor skills required to ride a bicycle).

Declarative memory involves four stages: registering, storing, seeking and forgetting. Registering occurs at the moment of learning, when the brain finds itself with a new piece of declarative information. That moment when we learn or register a piece of information is as mysterious as it is complex. We know very little about the process, only that this bit of information is divided up into small pieces, each of which are sent to different parts of the brain.

A group of people was shown ten written words. That group were then divided into two subgroups. One subgroup was asked to concentrate on which words had diagonal shapes among their letters, and the other to think about the meaning of each word and to rate them on a scale of one to ten according to how much they liked or disliked the words. After a few minutes, each group was asked to write down all the words they could remember. The group that had been asked to think about the meaning of the words and whether they liked them remembered two or three times as many as those who merely looked at the shape of the letters. That is to say, the more elaborate the process of registering the information at the moment of learning, the longer the memory.

Charles Duell, director of the United States Patent and Trademarks Office in 1899, said: 'Everything that can be invented has been invented.' Grover Cleveland, in 1905, declared: 'Sensible and responsible women don't want to vote.' Robert Millikan, winner of the Nobel Prize for physics in 1923, said: 'There is no likelihood man can ever tap the power of the atom.' Lord Kelvin, president of the Royal Society in 1825 said: 'I can state flatly that heavier than air flying machines are impossible'. The tsar of Russia, remarking on what he considered was the failure of the locomotive, commented: 'Nobody will pay to travel from Berlin to Potsdam in an hour when in one day they can get there by horse for free'.

Another common feature of memory is that the search for information already registered and stored is more efficient when the conditions in which it was registered are replicated. This is known as context-based learning. If we learn something when we are feeling sad, we are more likely to remember it at some point in the future when we feel sad again. Also, the more focused we are when we learn the meaning of a piece of information, the more elaborate the process of registering it in our memory. In other words, if you are confronted with information you don't understand, there isn't much point in trying to memorise it.

The famous method of 'rote learning', which generally means understanding little about what you are learning, can be problematic in exams if you are asked, not to remember, but to elaborate or relate the information to something else. It has also been shown that a good way of remembering things is to use examples from real life or familiar situations. The more personal the example the better; the easier it is to retrieve afterwards. When conveying information to others, the ability to create a good introduction to your subject is probably one of the most important factors in determining the success of your mission to teach or communicate. This is because the more neural structures involved at the moment of learning, the easier it is afterwards to access information and retrieve it.

It is estimated that at least once a week we experience the sensation of having something 'on the tip of our tongue'. Interestingly, this hiccup in our memory is accompanied by a deep conviction that we know whatever it is. This is why we make so much effort and use up a lot of mental energy trying to recall that word, name or idea. The mind has a natural ability to diagnose our problems and work out the kind of creativity they require. This 'feeling of knowing' (FOK), as it is called, convinces us that if we go on thinking about a problem we will eventually find a solution. Some studies show that when we are faced with problems that don't require insights, our mind is very clear about how we should confront and resolve them. Simply by understanding your challenge, you know that if you set to work you will obtain the best result, and that inspires you to concentrate on it. On the other hand, if you feel that you aren't making headway with your challenge, that you have reached an impasse, the chances are you need an insight; when that happens, continuing to concentrate and waste energy is pointless, you need to relax in order to increase your alpha waves. The most productive thing you can do is to forget about your challenge.

Old new memories

The process of converting short-term memory into long-term or durable memory is called consolidation. We now know that there is a clear link between repetition and memory. The best way to remember something for longer (consolidation) is by purposefully exposing yourself to it repeatedly.

At first, memory is extremely flexible, unstable and prone to extinction. Most stimuli and information we encounter in any given day fall into that category. As with short-term declarative or non-declarative memory, there are different types of long-term memory. Scientists still disagree as to the existence of all these different forms, but they do accept that there is a system of semantic memory which can record, for example, what your mother's favourite cake is, or how much you weighed when you were at primary school. They also describe something called episodic memory, which is responsible for recalling episodes from your past: what happened, who was there, where you were, etc. We also know that learning is far more effective when new information is incorporated gradually into the memory rather than all at once. And what about forgetting? Forgetting plays a vital role in our ability to function and enables us to prioritise. All those events that have no bearing on our survival take up a huge amount of space in our brain, and we instantly forget them. So, without going into detail about the different processes of forgetting, the way they all habitually work is to discard one piece of information to make way for another.

As we saw earlier, memory doesn't only make us human, it also plays a vital role in our survival. Being able to register and store the experiences of a lifetime forms the basis for all the ideas contained in our head. Remember that creativity, or the creative ideas we have, are simply the mixture of concepts, experiences, information, data, and apparently unrelated knowledge that has been stored somewhere in our memory. We have learned or experienced these concepts at some point, after which they have been carefully stored by our memory in neural 'drawers', mostly in our unconscious. Remember Eric Kandel's theory of intelligent memory in chapter three.

The unconscious learns first

Imagine four decks of cards, two red and two blue. The cards are face down, and the decks lined up in a row. When we turn over the cards, we see a sentence telling us whether we have won or lost varying amounts of money. The game consists of turning over the cards in order to win the most money possible. What the players don't know is that the winnings from the red decks are greater, but so are the losses, so that you can only win money if you pick cards from the blue decks, which offer more modest winnings as well as losses.

The question is how many cards on average do people have to turn over in order to understand that they can only win money from the blue decks? This experiment is known as the Iowa Gambling Task and was carried out in several different countries. Analysis of the results suggested that people start to realise 'something is wrong' when they get to about card number fifty; at that moment they instinctively start selecting cards from the blue decks, although seemingly without rhyme or reason. Only when they turn over the eightieth card are they able to explain what is happening and why. This is how our logic works. We acquire experience, then reflect on it, we elaborate a theory and finally we draw a conclusion. This is also how we learn.

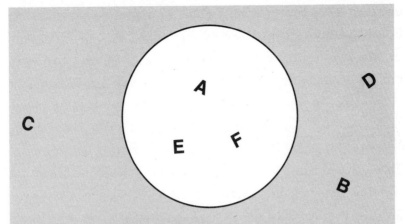

Can you work out quickly which of the missing letters of the alphabet should go outside and which inside the circle? If you assume that this is going to be a complex intellectual riddle that requires figuring out a system, you will fail. The solution is as simple as the structure or shape of the letters. Those that are rounded, like 'B', 'C' and 'D' will go outside the circle and those with straight lines will go inside. If your intuition is well developed, you will only have needed to glance at the letters to come up with the correct solution.

The same experiment is repeated with the participants' palms hooked up to a machine which measures perspiration – a sign of stress and anxiety. Around card number ten, stress signals are registered when a card is taken from the red deck. Forty cards before we become aware that 'something was wrong'! At that moment, still without realising, we start to pick more cards from the blue than from the red decks. In other words, *we discover that the game is rigged before we are consciously aware of it, and we start* making the necessary adjustments (picking more blue than red cards) without knowing we are doing it.

We can conclude from this that the brain uses two very different strategies in order to understand the situation: a conscious, more familiar strategy, in which we think about what we have learned and come up with a logical, cogent but slow response that requires a great deal of information (card no. eighty); and another, quick strategy which grasps the deception with the red pack almost at once, but which, inconveniently for us, works just below the level of consciousness, to begin with in any case, although it sends us messages by indirect means, in this case sweaty palms. *Our brain is drawing conclusions without telling us.* This last strategy, what psychologist Gerd Gigerenzer calls 'fast and frugal', is known in neuroscience as the 'adaptive unconscious' (not to be confused with Freud's obscure, murky subconscious, filled with desires, memories and fantasies which are so disturbing we can't think about them consciously).

Our adaptive unconscious is like a supercomputer processing quickly and silently the vast amounts of data we need to continue acting like human beings. For example, if we are crossing the road and a lorry bears down on us, we haven't time to think about all the different ways in which we might save our lives. In that situation, our adaptive unconscious will make a snap decision based on a rapid appraisal of very little information. The adaptive unconscious is a sensor that succeeds in getting an idea of our surroundings, warning us of dangers, establishing objectives, and initiating well-thought-out, efficient actions. What's more, depending on the situation, we humans can switch rapidly from conscious to unconscious mode. Let's imagine an example: if I invite you over to my house for dinner, I am making a conscious decision based on my desire to chat with you and because I think it would be fun. However, during the meal we might spontaneously, unconsciously start to discuss politics. This is carried out by a different part of the brain. Generally speaking, we use our adaptive unconscious when we meet someone for the first time, when we interview someone for a job, when we respond to a new diet or when we make a rapid decision under enormous pressure.

Dr Nalini Ambady carried out a classic experiment which looked at the important role our adaptive unconscious plays in decision-making. She showed a group of students three ten-minute recordings of different professors teaching a class, but without any sound, and then asked them to give the professors a mark. Astonishingly, the marks the professors obtained at the end of the semester didn't differ much from the students' evaluation. Even more incredibly, when the students were shown the videos for just five seconds, the marks they gave were identical. Further proof of the enormous power of the adaptive unconscious.

Professor George Turin of the University of California suggests that the different components used in solving problems intuitively might be:

1) We have the ability to know how to tackle a problem without knowing how we know.

2) We have the ability to solve a problem in one area because we have already solved similar problems in completely different

Continued

areas. We have the ability to see connections between ideas and objects.

3) We have the ability to see what the real root of a problem is.

4) We have the ability to recognise a solution simply because we 'feel' it is right.

If when confronted with a challenge you feel that you have those abilities, it means your intuition is highly developed. If not, you can use the techniques and exercises in this book to develop it more.

We have just seen, through the Iowa experiment, how part of our brain, our adaptive unconscious, acts below the threshold of consciousness. We make important decisions about our surroundings and ourselves without realising we are doing it. However, we also learned that that part of the brain sends us messages; by making our palms sweat, it 'speaks', or whispers to us in some way. Often, learning to listen to what our unconscious is trying to tell us helps us to know ourselves better and to become more aware of ourselves. Remember that what the most creative men and women in history have in common is a high level of self-knowledge, what we know today as 'intrapersonal emotional intelligence'. Unfortunately, the adaptive unconscious doesn't speak to us in the rational language of thought. It communicates in a different way, through mental states. Understanding better what state, or states, of mind we are in when confronted with different situations and at different moments of the day, or in our lives in general, enables us to improve our self-knowledge, and helps us to be able to decide, for example, whether it is useful to act. Let's separate these states into four.

Learning to listen to yourself

The first state is emotional. Feelings like dissatisfaction, irritability and frustration, which interfere with our performance at work or at home, in contrast to desired emotional states like joy, contentment, playfulness and curiosity. As we saw earlier, our emotions are strongly connected with the processes of our unconscious. The second state is emotional and physical: our brain gives us information about how our body feels: stressed, tense, tired or comfortable, flexible and relaxed. The third state is mental: what is going on in your head, are you thinking clearly, are you focused, confident and sure of yourself, open to new ideas? Or is your mind noisy, distracted, and stuck on one solution? And, finally, the fourth, spiritual state. Here I will leave it up to the reader to express his or her own experiences and definitions of spirituality. They might be religious or simply about understanding whether one is connected to oneself, to one's work, to the world, to other people, to one's creative challenge, or not.

What's clear is that these four states are in constant flux, depending on outside stimuli as well as internal processes, conscious or unconscious. The best way to check what state you are in is to relax, take three slow, deep breaths, and try to note what you feel in each of the four states described above, categorising them. That is one way of connecting with yourself, and being aware of when your mental processes discover something interesting. Similarly, when you are more alert to your sensations and responses to certain stimuli, you will feel more connected, and therefore better able to make the right decisions and feel easy about them. A clear example of this is when people describe intuitions and how they manifest themselves: they are interpreting changes in these states ('it sent a shiver down my spine', 'I broke out in a cold sweat', 'my heart leapt into my throat', etc.). When you notice these states, the best thing is to stop and explore them, because they are trying to tell you something. Remember that the more sensitive you are to understanding and detecting these states, the more aware you become.

In short: most of the information we receive from the outside world through different stimuli goes to our unconscious brain, and only a tiny fragment goes to our conscious brain. We could say that our conscious is small, very noisy and not very capable, compared to our unconscious, which is immensely capable and apparently silent. The vast flow of information we receive continually is, as we saw earlier, captured by our senses.

The shy person and the dominant person

Richard Wiseman uses a fascinating analogy to show the relationship between the conscious, the unconscious and creativity.

Two people are in a room. One is very creative but extremely shy; the other is intelligent, very dominant but less creative. A third person approaches them to ask for their ideas about a specific challenge. Predictably, the more dominant person will start to generate ideas, which aren't bad, but aren't particularly innovative or creative. He or she will control the conversation, preventing the shy person from contributing much. Now imagine the same scene, only this time the dominant person is distracted because he or she is watching a film. In this situation, the shy, creative person is able to make themselves heard, and his or her ideas are far more creative than those of the dominant person. This is a good analogy of the relationship between the mind and creativity. The shy person represents our unconscious, which is capable of producing amazing ideas but often remains unheard, and the dominant person represents our conscious mind, intelligent but not particularly innovative and difficult to blot out.

Intuition

Charles Merrill, of Merrill Lynch, said once that when he makes quick decisions, sixty percent of the time they are the correct ones. But if he takes the time to analyse the situation and reach a considered decision, that increases to seventy percent. Not a huge difference, certainly not one that Charles thinks is worth the loss of time required to think attentively.

We can practise, develop and improve our intuitive ability.

However, if you listen to your intuition, think logically about the situation and then combine those two processes, you achieve a powerful end result.

EXERCISE

Try to guess how a situation is going to turn out before analysing it in depth.

EXERCISE

Ask yourself questions to which you already know the answer, and reply to yourself with a yes or a no.

Continued

For example: Is it my birthday today? Is my mother's name Silvia? Is tomorrow Friday? Do I like the book I'm reading? Etc.

Be aware of what happens in your head when you reply 'yes' or 'no'. When you say 'yes' do you see flashing lights, the colour green, arrows? And when you say 'no' do you see red crosses, darkness?

Concentrate on the way your mind receives the information. The idea is to try to know yourself better, your way of saying 'yes' or 'no'. You are training yourself with familiar situations. Gradually you will start to see that when questions arise to which you don't know the answers, your intuition will start sending you similar signals (arrows, crosses, colours, etc.)

EXERCISE

The telephone rings. Without looking, try to guess who is calling. A man? A woman? A colleague? A relative? Is it a normal, everyday call? Or something different? Is it local or from abroad? Etc. You leave for work. How will things go for you at work today? Will you make lots of sales? Will you sell nothing? Which colours will sell more? Where will the bus overtake? Will there be a strike? Etc.

You arrive at work. Before opening your email, ask yourself: how many emails will I get today? How many of them will be junk mail, from my family, work related? How many will be strange, different or unexpected?

Go to sleep it's almost over

Nothing beats a good night's sleep, as they say. We feel fresh and ready to face the day. We all know that insomnia or lack of sleep can affect our mood and even our stress levels. Bed isn't just about pleasant sensations; sleep is good for learning and memory, among other things. Studies of animals show that sleep increases brain connections during early development. For example, cats that experience an environmental challenge, and are then allowed to sleep for six hours develop twice as many connections as cats that are kept awake.

What happens when we sleep? In 1965, a seventeen-year-old youth, called Randy Gardner, decided to try to stay awake for eleven days in a row for a class study at school. The researcher, William Dement, attended Randy during that period and noticed the following effects. After the first few days, his brain started to malfunction, Randy was irritable, nauseous, forgetful and, of course, exhausted. On the fifth day, his symptoms might easily have been mistaken for those of a patient with Alzheimer's; he was hallucinating, disoriented and paranoid. During the final four days of the experiment, he lost his motor function, his fingers shook and he could barely speak. Amazingly, he achieved his objective but he was in a deplorable state.

Undoubtedly, sleep is as crucial to us as water and air. We spend a third of our lives asleep. And yet, science still doesn't know exactly why we need it so much. If we could get inside someone's head, we would see that their brain never appears to sleep; not only that, even when in resting mode it remains highly active. The only time when the brain is silent and uses up less energy is during rapid eye movement sleeps (REMS), the deepest sleep phase. This phase takes up about twenty percent of our sleep, fifty percent in babies. Strictly speaking, we could say that the brain is still active even when it is asleep. Other parts of the body do rest when we sleep. If we consider sleep in evolutionary terms, there must be something extremely important about it, because out on the African plain, it meant being totally at the mercy of predators.

'When you don't use a muscle, that muscle really isn't doing much of anything... But when your brain is supposedly doing nothing and daydreaming, it's really doing a tremendous amount.'

Marcus Raichle

Some experiments have shown that driving when you haven't slept all night is as dangerous as driving drunk. Others that highly strung, anxious people tend to sleep a lot less in moments of crisis or stress, whereas those who ignore their emotions and focus more on tasks, sleep more than usual during such periods.

Who hasn't had a boyfriend or girlfriend who liked to go to bed early while we could easily have stayed up until two or three in the morning watching a film or out at a bar? Or vice versa. Scientific studies show that one-tenth of the population are morning types. These people wake up before six without an alarm clock, prefer breakfast to lunch and almost never drink coffee, but they go to bed at nine at night and their peak of productivity during the day is a few hours before lunch. I am not a morning type. Two out of every ten people are evening types; they never go to bed before 3 a.m., and without an alarm clock, they would carry on sleeping until at least ten in the morning. They are avid coffee drinkers, are most productive at around six in the evening and, of course, their favourite meal is dinner. Unfortunately, evening types accumulate a massive sleep deficit during their lifetime. The rest of us are somewhere between the two extremes. Sleep cycles vary between different people, according to age, sex, whether they are pregnant or going through puberty. However, we do know the minimum amount of sleep we need. The answer isn't very precise: if you wake up and feel you need to sleep a little longer, that amount of time, added to the hours you have already slept is the minimum amount of sleep you need so that nothing bad happens to your brain.

For a long time, scientists thought that the feeling of wanting to take a nap in the afternoon was related to a lack of sleep or eating a heavy lunch. Some scientists now believe that a good night's sleep plus a short afternoon nap is the natural sleep pattern in humans. Tests on NASA pilots showed that a twenty-six minute nap improved their performance by thirty percent, and another study has shown that a forty-five minute nap improves cognitive performance for six hours afterwards.

Whenever I have to give a talk after lunch, I know it will be a struggle.

The well-known expression 'I'll sleep on it' is backed up by hundreds of publications, which show that a good night's sleep increases our ability to learn when carrying out certain tasks, and as we have seen, that makes us more likely to have insights.

Satisfaction

An increasing body of scientific evidence suggests that dreaming enables us to make astonishing connections. When we start to dream, we stop worrying about logic, truth and common sense. Instead of censoring the thoughts floating around inside our minds, we embrace the freedom of their associations. One night in May 1965, Keith Richards imagined in his sleep one of the most influential songs in the world of rock music '(I Can't Get No) Satisfaction'.

People who take an afternoon nap in which they dream score forty-five percent better in association tests than when they wake up in the morning. When we dream, the prefrontal cortex switches off, and we are exposed to a wealth of astonishing connections. Most of them will be of no use, but one of them might provide the solution to our challenge in the middle of the night.

Recent studies show that when we have a poor night's sleep, about a third of our body's capacity to utilise food is impaired, i.e. our ability to produce insulin and extract glucose, the brain's favourite food. One final study shows that the metabolism of a healthy thirty year old who is deprived of sleep for six nights in a row and who has only slept for four hours, resembles that of a sixty year old. It takes a week of sleeping properly for their system to return to normal.

So, if we want to be more productive, we need to promote the idea of short naps at work and flexible timetables for the thirty percent of people who are morning or evening people. If you have an exam, a good night's sleep is better for you than staying up half the night revising. New memories are formed when we are exposed to fresh information that requires learning, such as a list of words or a piece for piano. As we know, these memories are fragile and liable to be forgotten quickly. In order to be retained, they have to go through the process we saw earlier known as memory consolidation. This happens when the connections between neurons in different parts of the brain are strengthened. For many years it was thought that this process occurred over time. However, a series of experiments in 2005 at the Beth Israel Deaconess Medical Centre in Boston, showed that the time we spend sleeping plays an essential role in the preservation and consolidation of memory.

If we don't get enough sleep, we are more likely to experience stress, have a diminished ability to make decisions, and gain weight. And that's only the beginning. Lack of sleep has also been associated with an increased risk of heart attack.

To ensure you get a good night's sleep, try the following: fix regular hours for going to bed and getting up. The body becomes accustomed to daily routines. Don't drink caffeine in the eight hours prior to going to bed. Do aerobic exercise (walking, swimming, jogging) in the afternoon. Don't do it later than two hours before going to bed. Sleep in a well-ventilated room where you aren't exposed to sudden changes in temperature, and where you can shut out as much light as possible. If the room is too light, try using a sleeping mask. Don't use an alarm clock with big, luminous numbers. Use a white noise machine to block out any sounds that might disturb you. Alternatively you can use earplugs. If you don't fall asleep within half an hour of switching off the light, get up and perform a relaxing activity, Staying in bed, stressed out because you can't sleep only makes matters worse.

> ### Dalí
>
> What did Salvador Dalí do? He sat in a very comfortable armchair and placed a glass beside him on the floor and held a teaspoon in his hand above the glass. As he started to drop off, his hand relaxed and the sound of the teaspoon falling into the glass woke him up. Then he started to draw all the strange images that had appeared in his head during the semiconscious state between sleep and wakefulness.

Everything must end, but only to begin again

What have we learned?

When we observe something we have already seen, we understand and give it a meaning. We do so without having to use up much time or energy analysing it. As we grow older, we accumulate thought patterns, habits and routines and, thanks to them, we are able to simplify things and carry out the majority of our daily tasks quickly and efficiently.

In order to be creative, we need to generate variations through combining or blending different concepts that change these thought patterns, providing us with fresh alternatives. Blending these different concepts will spark our imagination. Creative people don't think up amazing ideas because they are more intelligent, or because they are better educated and more experienced, or because they are genetically more predisposed to being creative. They simply combine different concepts in novel ways. That is the most important tool for generating more and more new ideas. They invest time and 'intention' on developing their creative energy, focusing their attention on their creative challenge. They enjoy the process and they are curious.

In fact, every time we feel, see, think, speak or decide to move our body, a unique pattern, a specific network of neurons is activated. Those neurons connect with one another through synapses or neurotransmitters. For example, when we see a car, this activates one specific neural network, and if we hear a dog bark, a different network is activated. Broadly speaking, to think creatively means to activate a completely new, unique neural network. And it is by studying these structures and their characteristics, how they are constructed, that we can start to understand more and more about the thought process in general.

Relaxation is not for me

If the idea of being relaxed is too difficult or abstract for you to imagine, try instead to feel a sensation of heat and heaviness. In a comfortable position, with your eyes closed, imagine that your hands, arms and legs are growing heavier and heavier, warmer and warmer.

There is no need to think about the word relaxation; replace it with heaviness and heat, and that will help you to relax.

There is no doubt that creativity is one of the most important tools for human survival and evolution. And yet, it is often considered by society as a rather superfluous gift. Far more emphasis is placed on our ability to rationalise. If we wish to develop our creativity as much as possible, our schools should include and promote activities associated with it on their curricula. When we are adults, the world appears to be made up of important responsibilities and decisive actions. And yet we often confuse what is important with what is serious. When was the last time you were attacked by a leopard? The actions we take may be decisive, but they are scarcely situations that require swift evaluation, an instant fight or flight response.

More often than not, the challenges we face require different ways of thinking. We ourselves can cultivate and promote this. We need a cultural change, one that embraces other values, and where a sense of play is also encouraged in adults. We need to promote activities that have no impact on our lives, our careers, our finances, our lifestyle or societal relations. We need to stop being so correct and try to enjoy doing something just for the sake of it. When we were small, we instinctively took everything we could from our surroundings, instead of behaving properly or with caution. Over time, our defence mechanisms started to play a bigger role, and to emphasise the need to be cautious and correct, to avoid any kind of emotional or physical pain. We became serious, pragmatic creatures. Music, theatre, art and games became purely recreational activities. And yet now, neuroscience understands that all those activities develop our creative muscles.

The creation of new associations or concepts in our mind generally occurs when we have a space in which to relax, when the influence of pre-existing dominant neural connections subsides. Apart from scientific discoveries, all the world's great traditions from time immemorial have emphasised the need to live lives that weaken a little the hold of those dominant thought patterns. Taoism encourages people to live simpler lives. The essence of Tao is to attempt to go with the flow, instead of constantly trying to control every aspect of our lives. Buddhism places great emphasis on the need to be aware of our thoughts, and careful in our actions, so that we aren't caught up in habitual thoughts and desires. Hindus and Yogis preach letting go of our desires. The more western practices of forgiveness and faith also promote and achieve freedom from dominant thought patterns. All these traditions teach us to accept what is now and abandon our need to control things we cannot. We needn't live as if every situation were a matter of life and death. Living in that way weakens our stress mechanisms, which are vital when we find ourselves facing a dangerous situation.

We have a tendency to associate creative thinking with special projects, an important challenge at work, an art installation, an invention, improved productivity, solving a design problem for a new product. And yet, in our everyday lives, away from these big challenges, we continue using the same dominant thought patterns; we experience and respond to situations on automatic pilot. It is necessary to compensate for this mechanism of automatic decision-making with creative thinking.

Thinking creatively, through insight, provides us with the opportunity to evolve continually as humans, which is particularly important today in the increasingly complex the world we have built.

In order to benefit from this evolutionary gift, we must become more aware that we operate in our lives, our finances, our careers, our relationships on automatic pilot. We complain that we have no time to stop, re-evaluate our actions and live a more creative life, and yet all the shortcuts we take in life, on automatic pilot, often take longer, causing us to behave inefficiently; we make mistakes and we suffer. Thinking creatively is the only way for us to live our own lives and not that of others.

In my view, we can only claim to be truly alive when, instead of giving the habitual responses, we allow ourselves the possibility to make decisions through a conscious process. We can only do this if we live more creatively.

'Hell is a place where nothing connects with nothing.'

T. S. Eliot

'Your time is limited, so don't waste it living someone else's life. Don't be trapped by dogma – which is living with the results of other people's thinking.'

Steve Jobs

Mental maps

Mental maps are one of the easiest and most powerful tools for freeing your creative potential. They were created by the British researcher, Tony Buzan, who was inspired by the works of Leonardo da Vinci. Nowadays, mental maps are a key element of courses and methods used in schools and organisations for problem-solving and learning. They can be used for personal aims such as planning a holiday or study regime, as well as preparing presentations or meetings, or for setting goals at work. But the best thing about them is that using them frequently trains your mind so that you become a more balanced thinker (using both sides of your brain), like Leonardo da Vinci.

Imagine that you have to write a review of the last film you saw at the cinema. Observe how your mind works during the process. Does it write paragraphs about the film or does it describe and list the most significant passages? Almost certainly not. It is far more likely that the *impressions* the film made on you, *key words and images*, float around in your mind, associating with one another. Mental maps are a continuation of what your brain already does, only on paper, a graphic representation of natural thought patterns. Remember that the most amazing database in the world is in your head.

As we have already seen, creativity requires a balance between generating and organising new ideas, before selecting them as creative and feasible, or discarding them. What usually happens is that we suffer from 'premature organisation', i.e. we start to organise first at the expense of producing ideas. Mental maps free you from that tyranny. They encourage you to generate more ideas more quickly, and enable you to represent an enormous amount of information in a reduced space. You can display all key concepts of a subject in such a way that it stimulates you to find connections between them. It is precisely this ability to discover connections between ideas that makes us more our creative. Besides being a powerful tool to improve your efficiency in resolving problems, planning, and communicating, I believe that the most important benefit of mental maps is that they train you to become a more flexible thinker. Regular use of mental maps develops your spontaneity, clarity and depth of thought, and, last but not least, you enjoy yourself while you are working and resolving creative challenges.

Mental mapping

Start with the biggest sheet of blank paper you can find, and five or six coloured marker pens or pencils. Spread the sheet of paper in front of you on a flat surface. In the centre of the piece of paper, draw or represent with a symbol the subject you are going to map as vividly as possible. Don't worry too much about how it looks. Use colours. After representing your main image, start to write down the ideas that best characterise it on lines radiating from the centre. Keep writing down key words and concepts until they begin to form a many-branched tree. Try to let your associations flow so that you fill the page as quickly as possible. Generating ideas in the form of key words is easy. When you feel you have generated enough material through free association, look at the result. All your ideas spread out on a page. As you examine it, you will start to see connections that will help you to organise and integrate your ideas. If you find you have repeated a word, that could mean something significant. Link up different parts of the map with arrows, codes and colours. Remove any sections that don't seem alien.

Be sure to use as many images as possible, because they serve as anchors for your key words. Try to use just one word per line, as that will train and discipline you to focus on finding the right word, strengthening your thinking. A mental map can go on forever: it ends when you have generated enough information to achieve your goals.

BIBLIOGRAPHY

Books

Ackerman, Diane, *A Natural History of the Senses*, New York, Vintage, 1991.

Ambady, Nalini, *First Impressions*, New York, The Guilford Press, 2008.

Andreasen, Nancy, *The Creating Brain: The Neuroscience of Genius*, New York, Dana Press, 2011.

Bateson, Gregory, *Steps to an Ecology of Mind: Collected Essays in Anthropology, Psychiatry, Evolution, and Epistemology*, Chicago, University of Chicago Press, 2000.

Begley, Sharon, *Train your mind, Change your brain: how a new science reveals our extraordinary potential to transform ourselves*, New York, Ballantine Books, 2007.

Birdwhistell, Ray, *Kinesics and Context: Essays on Body Motion Communication*, Pennsylvania, University of Pennsylvania Press, 1970.

Blakeslee, Sandra, *The Body Has a Mind of its Own*, New York, Random House, 2007.

Brook, Peter, *The Empty Space: A Book About the Theatre: Deadly, Holy, Rough, Immediate*, New York, Touchstone, 1995.

Buzan, Tony, *El poder de la inteligencia creativa*, México, Urano, 2003.

Carpenter, Malcolm and Sutin, Jerome, *Human Neuroanatomy*, London, Williams & Wilkins, 1976.

Carter, Rita, *The Human Brain Book*, London, DK ADULT, 2009.

Christensen, Clayton, *The Innovator's DNA: Mastering the Five Skills of Disruptive Innovators*, Boston, Harvard Business Review Press, 2011.

Csikszentmihalyi, Mihaly, *Creativity: Flow and the Psychology of Discovery and Invention*, London, Harper Perennial, 1997.

Csikszentmihalyi, Mihaly, *Fluir: Una psicología de la felicidad*, Barcelona, Editorial Kairós, 1997.

Damasio, Antonio, *El Error de Descartes*, Madrid, Crítica, 2008.

Dawkins, Richard, *El genegoísta: Las bases biológicas de nuestra conducta*, Barcelona, Salvat, 2009.

De Bono, Edward, *Creatividad: 62 ejercicios para desarrollar la mente*, Barcelona, Paidós Ibérica Ediciones, 2008.

DeLoache, Judy, *How Children Develop*, Boston, Worth Publishers, 2010.

Dement, William, *The Promise of Sleep: A Pioneer in Sleep Medicine Explores the Vital Connection Between Health, Happiness, and a Good Night's Sleep*, New York, Dell, 2000.

Deutsch, George and Springer, Sally, *Cerebro izquierdo, cerebro derecho*, Barcelona, Gedisa, 2008.

Diamond, David, *Theatre For Living: The Art and Science of Community-Based Dialogue*, Bloomington IN, Trafford Publishing, 2007.

Dickinson, Emily, *Poemas*, Abington PA, Visor, 2000.

Doidge, Norman, *The Brain That Changes Itself: Stories of Personal Triumph from the Frontiers of Brain Science*, London, Penguin, 2007.

Duggan, William, *Strategic Intuition: The Creative Spark in Human Achievement*, New York, Columbia University Press, 2007.

Fisher, Helen, *Why Him? Why Her?: Finding Real Love By Understanding Your Personality Type*, New York, Henry Holt and Co., 2009.

Florida, Richard, *The Rise of the Creative Class: And How It's Transforming Work, Leisure, Community, and Everyday Life*, New York, Basic Books, 2003.

Foster, Jack, *How to Get Ideas*, San Francisco, Berrett-Koehler Publishers, 2007.

Galindo, Javy, *The Power of Thinking Differently: An imaginative guide to creativity, change, and the discovery of new ideas*, Los Altos, Hyena Press, 2011.

Gelb, Michael, *Da Vinci Decodificado*, Madrid, Punto de Lectura, 2006.

Gelb, Michael, *Descorche su creatividad*, Colombia, Grupo Editorial Norma, 2010.

Gelb, Michael and Caldicott, Sarah, *Innovate Like Edison: The Five-Step System for Breakthrough Business Success*, New York, Plume, 2008.

Gigerenzer, Gerd, *Decisiones instintivas*, St. Harmon, Ariel, 2008.

Goleman, Daniel, *Espíritu creativo*, Barcelona, Ediciones B, 2009.

Gordon, Evian and Koslow, Stephen, *Integrative Neuroscience and Personalized Medicine*, New York, Oxford University Press, 2010.

Gross, James, *Handbook of Emotion Regulation*, New York, The Guilford Press, 2009.

Hebb, D.O., *The Organization of Behavior: A Neuropsychological Theory*, London, Psychology Press, 2002.

Kandel, Eric, *In Search of Memory: The Emergence of a New Science of Mind*, Nueva York, W. W. Norton & Company, 2007.

Kandel, Eric, *The Age of Insight: The Quest to Understand the Unconscious in Art, Mind, and Brain, from Vienna 1900 to the Present*, New York, Random House, 2012.

Kaufman, James and Sternberg, Robert, *The Cambridge Handbook of Creativity*, Cambridge, Cambridge University Press, 2010.

LeDoux, Joseph, *El cerebro emocional*, St. Harmon, Ariel Publications, 1999.

Lehrer, Jonah, *Imagine: How Creativity Works*, Boston, Houghton Mifflin Harcourt, 2012.

Lippmann, Walter, *Essays in the Public Philosophy*, New York, The New American Library, 1964.

Lynch, David, *Atrapa el pez dorado: Meditación, conciencia y creatividad*, Barcelona, Grijalbo Mondadori, 2008.

MacLean, P., *The Triune Brain in Evolution: Role in Paleocerebral Functions*, New York, Springer, 1999.

MacLeod, Hugo, *Ignora a todos (Gestión del conocimiento)*, México, Urano, 2010.

Mayer, Richard, *Aprendizaje e instrucción*, Madrid, Alianza Editorial, 2010.

Medina, John, Brain Rules: 12 Principles for Surviving and Thriving at Work, Home, and School, Seattle, Pear Press, 2009.

Meltzoff, Andrew, Palabras, pensamientos y teoría, Madrid, Visor, 2002.

Michalko, Michael, Creative Thinkering: Putting Your Imagination to Work, San Francisco, New World Library, 2011.

Michalko, Michael, Thinkertoys, México, Gestión 2000, 2001.

Michalko, Michael, Cracking creativity: Los secretos de los genios de la creatividad, México, Gestión 2000, 2000.

Pfenninger, Karl and Shubik, Valerie, The Origins of Creativity, New York, Oxford University Press, 2001.

Pinker, Steven, Cómo funciona la mente, Madrid, Destino, 2000.

Pradeep, A.K., The Buying Brain: Secrets for Selling to the Subconscious Mind, New Jersey, Wiley, 2010.

Raina, M., The Creativity Passion: E. Paul Torrance's Voyages of Discovering Creativity, Praeger, 2000.

Ramachandran, V. S., The Tell-Tale Brain: A Neuroscientist's Quest for What Makes Us Human, New York, W. W. Norton & Company, 2011.

Restak, Richard and Kim, Scott, The Playful Brain: The Surprising Science of How Puzzles Improve Your Mind, New York, Riverhead Hardcover, 2010.

Rizzolatti, Giacomo, Las neuronas espejo: Los mecanismos de la empatía emocional, Madrid, Paidós Ibérica Ediciones, 2006.

Rock, David, Your Brain at Work: Strategies for Overcoming Distraction, Regaining Focus, and Working Smarter All Day Long, New York, HarperBusiness, 2009.

Roth, Robert, Meditación trascendental de Maharishi Mahesh Yogi, Edición Estándar, 2003.

Rothenberg, Albert, Creativity and Madness: New Findings and Old Stereotypes, Baltimore, The Johns Hopkins University Press, 1990.

Sloterdijk, Peter, Temperamentos filosóficos: De Platón a Foucault, Madrid, Siruela, 2010.

Sperry, Roger, Beyond a World Divided: Human Values in the Brain-Mind Science, Bloomington, iUniverse, 2000.

Sternberg, Robert, The Nature of Creativity: Contemporary Psychological Perspectives, Cambridge, Cambridge University Press, 1988.

Sweeney, Michael, *Brain: The Complete Mind: How It Develops, How It Works, and How to Keep It Sharp*, Washington, National Geographic, 2009.

Todd, James, *Modern Perspectives on John B. Watson and Classical Behaviorism*, Westport, Greenwood Press, 1994.

Wilson, Edward, *Consilience: The unity of knowledge*, New York, Random House/Vintage Books, 1999.

Wiseman, Richard, *El factor suerte*, Madrid, Temas de Hoy, 2003.

Creativity Test, adapted from the blog of Josh Linkner: http://joshlinkner.com/blog

Scientific articles

Armstrong, E., "Relative Brain Size and Metabolism in Mammals", in *Science* 220, no. 4603 (June 17, 1983), 1302–1304.

Arp, R, "The environments of our hominid ancestors, tool-usage and scenario visualization", in *Biol & Phil* 21: 95–117 (2006).

Benoit, O. et al., "Habitual sleep length and patterns of recovery sleep after 24 hour and 36 hour sleep deprivation", in *Electroencephogr Clin Neurophysiol* 50: 477–485 (1980).

Braver, T.S. et al., "Neural mechanisms of transient and sustained cognitive control during task switching", in *Neuron* 39: 713–26 (2003).

Burns, E.R., "Biological time and in vivo research: a field guide to pitfalls", in *Anat Rec* 261: 141–152 (2000).

Cole, W. et al., "The Multitasking Generation", in *Time* 167: 50–53 (2006).

Crone, E.A. et al., "Neural evidence for dissociable components of task-switching", in *Cereb Cortex* 16: 475–86 (2006).

Culotta, E. et al., "Paleolithic technology and human evolution" in *Science* 291: p. 1748–1753 (2001).

DeLoache et al., "Scale errors offer evidence for a perception-action dissociation early in life", in Science 304: 1027–1029 (2004).

DeLoache, JD., "Becoming symbol-minded", in *Trends in Cognitive Sciences* 8(2):66–70 (2004).

Dinges, DF. et al., "Cumulative sleepiness, mood disturbance, and psychomotor vigilance performance decrements during a week of sleep restricted to 4–5 hours per night", in *Sleep* 20: 267–277 (1997).

Dolcos, F. et al., "Interaction between the amygdala and the medial temporal lobe memory system predicts better memory for emotional events", in *Neuron* 42: 855–863 (2004).

Dunbar et al., "Evolution in the social brain" in *Science* 317:1344–1347 (2007).

Endestad, T. et al., "Memory for pictures and words following literal and metaphorical decisions Imagination", in *Cognition and Personality* 23 (2,3): 209–216 (2003).

Gale, G. and Martin, C., "Larks and owls, and health, wealth, and wisdom", in *British Med J.* 317: 1675–1677 (1998).

Gottfried, J., Dolan R., "The nose smells what the eye sees: crossmodal visual facilitation of human olfactory perception", in *Neuron* 39: 375–386 (2003).

Gulevich, G. et al., "Psychiatric and EEG observations on a case of prolonged (264 hrs) wakefulness", in *Archives of General Psychiatry* 15: 29–35 (1966).

Hidi, S., and Baird, W., "Strategies for increasing text-based interest and student's recall of expository text", in *Reading Research Quarterly* 23: 465–483 (1988).

Hoffman, C.D. and Dick, S.A., "A developmental investigation of recognition memory", in *Child Dev* 47: 794–799 (1976).

Jacobs, W. et al., "The molecular basis of neural regeneration", in *Neurosurgery* 53: 943–950 (2003).

Larson, J et al., "Morning and night couples: the effect of wake and sleep patterns on marital adjustment", in *J. Marital and Fam Therapy* 17: 53–65 (1991).

Lewis, M. D., "The self-regulating brain: Cortical-subcortical feedback and the development of intelligence action", in *Cognitive Development* 22:406–430, 2005.

Lieberman, M.D., "Social cognitive neuroscience: a review of core processes", in *Annu Rev Psychol* 2007; 58:259–89 (2007).

Mayer, R.E., "Multimedia learning: are we asking the right questions?", in *Educ Psych* 32(1): 1–19 (1997).

Pelli, D.G., "The remarkable inefficiency of word recognition", in *Nature* 423: 752–756 (1996).

Pihal, W., and Born, J., "Effects of early and late nocturnal sleep on declarative and procedural memory", in *J. Cogn. Neurosci* 9: 534–547 (1997).

Pilcher, J.J. and Juffcutt A.J., "Effects of sleep deprivation on performance: a meta-analysis", in *Sleep* 19: 318–326 15: 29–35 (1996).

Ramsey, N.F. et al., "Neurophysiological factors in human information processing capacity", in *Brain* 127: 517–525 (2003).

Raz, A. y Buhle, J., "Typologies of attentional networks", in *Nature Reviews Neuroscience* 7: 367–379 (2006).

Repacholi, B.M. y Gopnik, A., "Early reasoning about desires: evidence from 14 and 18 month olds", in *Dev Psych* 33: 12–21 (1997).

Rizzolatti, G. and Craighero, L., "The mirror-neuron system", in *Ann Rev Neurosci* 27: 169–192.

Semaw et al., "2.5 million year old stone tools from Gona, Ethiopia", in *Nature* 385:333–336 (1997).

Silk et al., "Social components of fitness in primate groups", in *Science* 317:1347–1351 (2007).

Stenberg, G., "Conceptual and perceptual factors in the picture superiority effect", in *Eur J. of Cog Psych* 18(6): 813–847 (2006).

Stickgold, R., "Sleep-dependent memory consolidation", in *Nature* 437: 1272–1278 (2005).

Tanaka, J., "Protein Synthesis and neurotrophin-dependent structural plasticity of single dendritic spines", in *Science* 319:1683–1687, 2008.